THE *Trial* OF THE STICK OF JOSEPH

A Lecture Series by
JACK H. WEST

1981 Edition

Sounds OF ZION INCORPORATED

ISBN 1-886472-01-7

Second Printing 1985
Third Printing 1991
Fourth Printing 1994
Fifth Printing 1998
Sixth Printing 2001
Seventh Printing 2005

Sounds of Zion
9298 South 500 West
Sandy, UT 84070

www.soundsofzion.com

Contents

This is an actual transcript of three lectures given by Jack H. West on June 24th and 25th, 1954 at Brigham Young University. The text has been retained exactly as given, so that you, the reader, might have the feeling that you are right there, participating with the other class members. May you enjoy the informality, the change of pace, the sense of humor and the drama to be found in...

THE TRIAL OF THE STICK OF JOSEPH
BY
JACK H. WEST

S O THAT YOU may get started correctly, let me give you a little background on *The Trial of the Stick of Joseph*.

Many years ago when I was studying law in school, I had an old professor who had the peculiar notion that he should never give his students a written examination, but rather, should let them demonstrate their knowledge of law under conditions approximating those of a courtroom. Since he had been a judge for many years, he could devise courtroom conditions very similar to an actual case. So he notified each of us at the outset of that particular year's work that sometime during the year we would have, as he called it, the "privilege" of defending or prosecuting some case against the entire balance of the law class. If any of you studied law, I am sure you will agree that where there are many attorneys on the one side to do rapid and thorough research work, great advantage accrues against a lone individual on the other side.The individual standing alone did not have the advantage of many minds working as one.It seemed that what one of these young fellows in the group could not think of, someone else did.

I had absolutely no confidence in my own ability to either defend or prosecute any case I could think of against the entire balance of that law class. And so I was shaking in my boots, as were others in the class, over this type of test. While we found that most of these law cases lasted for only a day or two, or a week at the most, we got into one that ran for nearly three weeks.Here is further background of that one.

I had been studying and teaching the *Book of Mormon* simultaneously with my period of studying law. On the one hand I studied law, and on the other hand I studied the *Book of Mormon*. I became more and more convinced that God himself had briefed the case for the authenticity of that great book—the *Book of Mormon;* that He had set up the evidence, prepared the witnesses, and indeed He had made a complete case for the authenticity of that record. I found that he was doing exactly as the words of the book said, proving to all men that the words of that book were true. *(See 2 Nephi 11:3.)* So I thought to myself, "Well, Jack, if you are going to have a test and you do not feel able to stand up to that test, what better could you do than to get the Lord on your side?" So I took the case for the authenticity of the *Book of Mormon* or, as the Bible calls it, *The Stick of Joseph,* defending it and those who brought it forth, against a charge of fraud.

Gradually over the years, with no intention to develop the notes of this case into lecture form, the notes have grown into a group of three lectures. The first has to do with the examination of twelve personal witnesses who claimed to have seen and handled the ancient golden records from which Joseph Smith claimed to have translated the work. We will go into the lives of these men and see if they ever denied their testimonies and look at the peculiar circumstances surrounding their testimonies.

In the second lecture we go into internal evidence, to the book itself, letting it, so to speak, stand on its own two feet; we let it answer a whole group of charges made by the prosecution against the work. We find that it is its own best witness; that it will answer the charges in and of itself; that is consistent with itself; that it does not contradict itself nor the other great book, the "Stick of Judah," the *Bible*, which was to be its running mate.

In the third lecture we go to the very greatest men in the fields of science, having to do with the study of ancient races, particularly those men who have made a study of the ancient reaches of this continent—archaeologists, ethnologists, zoologists, anthropologists, and all kinds of "ologists," and from their testimonies we set up the external evidence for the authenticity of the *Book of Mormon*.

In the third session I will not quote one member of The Church of Jesus Christ of Latter-day Saints for fear someone might say, "Well, of course, he'd say that—he's a member of the Mormon Church." Rather, I will purposely stay with the greatest men in the fields of science who are not members of the Church and yet who have made in many cases a lifetime study of the ancient ruins for this continent, its peoples, their customs, languages, religion, and so forth.

–JACK H. WEST

ACT I
PERSONAL WITNESSES

(See written testimony in The Pearl of Great Price and the front few pages of the *Book of Mormon*)

KEY WITNESS	KEY	
JOSEPH SMITH		Beginning Spring of 1820—1st great vision - Father & Son
Born 1805	(3)	9-21-23—Moroni visions—next day Hill Cumorah, NY
Died a martyr	(4)	9-22-27—Receives plates and instrument to translate after 4 yearly visits
James 1:5		1830—*Book of Mormon* published

THREE SPECIAL WITNESSES	KEY	*Three Witnesses: 2 Nephi 27:12, Ether 5:2-3, D&C Sec. 17*
OLIVER COWDERY		Beginning 1829—Meets Joseph Smith
Born 1806	(9)	To 1838—Active, high offices, then excommunicated
	(10)	1848—10 years out of Church, bitter enemy of Joseph Smith readmitted after repentance
	(Life in)	Bears strong testimony until death.Tells story of vision—angel and voice of God. See signed testimony in the *Book of Mormon*
DAVID WHITMER		Beginning 1829—Meets Joseph Smith
Born 1805	(9)	To 1838—Active, high offices, then excommunicated
	(Life out)	never returned to the Church—In 1881, caused testimony to be printed in Ray Co., MO, *Conservator*. Reprinted in *New York Times* and *London Times*. 19 most famous men of MO testify to his honesty. At death bed he again reaffirms testimony
MARTIN HARRIS		Beginning 1827—Meets Joseph Smith
Born 1783	(10)	To 1837 —Until now very active in Church—the Church moves West and he remains behind
	(33)	Left "by himself"—Testimony never falters
	(Life in)	Finally comes to Utah. Thousands hear his ringing testimony

EIGHT OTHER WITNESSES	Read Testimony in front of *Book of Mormon*

CHRISTIAN WHITMER	HIRUM PAGE
JACOB WHITMER	JOSEPH SMITH, SR.
PETER WHITMER, JR.	HYRUM SMITH
JOHN WHITMER	SAMUEL H. SMITH

Joseph Smith Jr. showed plates to these men as one man would show something to any group of men—No display from heaven—broad daylight. These men handled and hefted golden record and turned pages with own hands—None ever denied—even though split up, some leaving Church—Becoming enemies. If this were a fraud—is it not strange that although most perfect conditions existed for a betrayal, none of them ever denied testimony?

DID WITNESSES HAVE ULTERIOR MOTIVES?
WERE THEY:
1. IMPOSTERS with intent to deceive for Power? ...Fame? ...Wealth?
   NO. Search of lives of witnesses shows that no motives for fraud existed.
2. ENTHUSIASTS—bitter enmity would have cooled enthusiasm in later years.
3. DELUDED—after Joseph Smith murdered, no longer able to influence.
4. TRUTHFUL—YES! It's the ONLY answer left.

ACT I
Personal Witnesses

AT THE OUTSET I asked the prosecution to turn to *Ezekiel* in the *Old Testament* to read something on which we base the very necessity of having a record called the Stick of Joseph or a record answering its description.

> The word of the Lord came again unto me, saying,
> Moreover, thou son of man, take thee one stick, and write upon it, For Judah, and for the children of Israel his companions: then take another stick, and write upon it, For Joseph, The stick of Ephraim, and for all the house of Israel his companions:
> And join them on to another into one stick; and they shall become one in thine hand. *(Evidently the Lord wanted to be sure that nobody misunderstood, so he repeated somewhat, in the next verse.)*
> And when the children of thy people shall speak unto thee, saying, Wilt thou not shew us what thou meanest by these?
> Say unto them, Thus saith the Lord God; Behold, I will take the **Stick of Joseph,** (Joseph of Israel) which is in the hand of Ephraim, and the tribes of Israel his fellows, and will put them with him, even with the stick of Judah, and make them one stick, and they shall be one in mine hand.
> *Ezekiel 37:15-19*

Here were to be two great records, not just one. How many tribes of Israel? Twelve. How many so-called lost tribes? Ten. We have a Stick of Joseph here—the *Book of Mormon,* and a Stick of Judah here—*The Bible.*

The prosecution said to me, "What is this 'stick' business?"

We went back into ancient times to show that those people did not have the printed page, as we know it today. They wrote on long strips of material, then rolled the material on a stick, and it became known as a stick of a "roll of a book." *(See Jeremiah 36:2; Ezekiel 2:9)*

What was the office of Ezekiel to whom the Lord was speaking? A prophet. And when God speaks to a prophet, the prophet writes those words, and they become what? Scripture! Then Ezekiel is telling us that these two sticks are to be scriptural records, one for the **tribe** of Joseph and of Israel and one for the tribe of Judah of Israel.

The parties of the prosecution said to me, "But the title of this book says the *Book of Mormon.*"

I said to them, "But this says *The Holy Bible,*" and they got the point.

Why do we of the Church know that the Bible is the Stick of Judah, and why did the court readily admit it was the Stick of Judah? Because the Bible tells about the tribe of Judah, and the only time it mentions any other tribe of Israel is as that tribe's history relates to the tribe of Judah.

"Of what tribe was Jesus Christ?"

"Judah."

"Then could the *New Testament* be the Stick of Joseph?"

"No."

I said to them, "Do you have the Stick of Joseph?" When I first mentioned it, they looked through their vest pockets, and they didn't seem to have it. They said, "But we can get it."

So they went to their rabbis and their ministers and their priests, and they came back empty-handed, and they said, "We don't have it."

I said, "Then would you object if I placed the Stick of Joseph in evidence as exhibit 'A' in this case? I testify to you that the *Book of Mormon* is the Stick of Joseph because if we read it, it tells about a segment of the **tribe of Joseph** and God's dealings with that tribe of Joseph on this, the American continent as we know it today."

The prosecution charged that not only was the Stick of Joseph, or the *Book of Mormon*, fraudulent in nature, but also that those who brought it forth—Joseph Smith, Oliver Cowdery, David Whitmer, Martin Harris, and others who had part in bringing this record forth and in testifying of its authenticity—were guilty of fraud.

At the conclusion of the case and upon the concluding arguments by both the prosecution and the defense, the judge rendered decision in favor of the defense. He said to the prosecution, "You have not even established a toe hold, much less a foothold, in breaking down the marvelous evidence for the authenticity of the Stick of Joseph (as we called it in the trial) much less have you given any evidence that would show it to be a fraudulent work."

Of course I was very happy about this, being the only member of the Church in the class. Then the judge called me into his office and said, "Jack, where in the world did you get the evidence you presented in this mock trial?" I grinned at him and said, "You remember at the outset of the trial I told all of you that I did not take credit for one particle of this evidence. Most of it has been available to the world for over a hundred years. And I told you then, as I tell you now, that I believe with all of my heart that God himself set up that evidence and prepared the witnesses."

The judge said, "I want to tell you something. In all of my years in law, I don't think I have heard a law case more nearly perfect than this one. When you started out, I wouldn't have given you a plugged nickel for your chances of proving that book to be true through legal procedure."

Brothers and sisters, don't sell the *Book of Mormon* short! I have had many people say to me, "Jack, I believe the *Book of Mormon* is true. I have a testimony of it, but I have always felt that I would be in a bad spot if somebody challenged many of the statements in it. I didn't think we could prove it with evidence that would stand up in an unbiased mind."

But you can! It doesn't take as much faith today to believe the *Book of Mormon* as it did when it came off the press in the year of 1830. Certainly there are still statements in it which are prophecy even now. They are still in the future as to fulfillment, but enough of the statements have been fulfilled that it takes less faith today to accept it than it did in the year 1830.

Now to the trial. We can't call the twelve witnesses to the *Book of Mormon* back in person. They have long since passed away. But we **can** call their **words** back, for on many occasions they gave their testimonies, sometimes under oath in courts of this land and they left their written testimony as well.

I want all of you to be completely relaxed and at ease, so I'll tell you that I'm going to call on twelve of you to come up here in front, one by one, to act as proxy witnesses so that we can better visualize the twelve personal witnesses to the *Book of Mormon*. None of you have been notified. Now isn't that a nice relaxing thought?—You won't have to say anything. You'll just sit here and look pretty.

First of all, in **personal witnesses,** I will call Joseph Smith the Prophet. Without him, the very key witness in our case, we have no case. If his testimony will not stand up, then none of it will. And if his testimony will stand up, we have a marvelous foundation for the balance of the testimonies.

Remember, the Prophet Joseph was tall, rather blond, had a marvelous physique, was renowned as a wrestler and was a fine-looking fellow. So I will ask Clair to come to the stand to act as "proxy" for Joseph Smith, because he looks so much like the Prophet. You can pay me later for that compliment, Clair.

Do you know that Joseph Smith, according to the testimony of Brigham Young and others, was a party to over fifty lawsuits? In searching, I found only twenty-seven. I say only twenty-seven, but that would be a lot for any one of us. I found, however, several places where court records had been destroyed by fire or by vandalism or by mobs. Undoubtedly the statement that Joseph Smith was a party to law case in over fifty suits is true. We can get his testimony sworn under oath from these cases. We also have his written testimony, and the testimony of those who were present when he made certain statements. And so we go to his testimony now to set up the evidence as to the coming forth of the *Book of Mormon*.

Joseph Smith's story was simple, and it was straightforward. The things implied were rather amazing, but still his story was simple. To what did he testify? Turning to his own words in what we have called "The Writing of Joseph Smith," a part of *The Pearl of Great Price*, we find that he begins by telling us that in his home area, nearby Manchester or Palmyra, in New York State, a religious revival took place. The Smith family had been living on what may be considered a western frontier in that day. There were just scattered farms and not enough families in many cases to organize official church groups. But more and more families came into this area, and several church ministers decided they would put on a "combined revival," as we call it today. The decision of the ministers, according to Joseph Smith's testimony, was that regardless of what church the various converts responded to, the clergymen would not get angry with each other. The Prophet said it all started in a very friendly way, but soon the revival program became filled with animosity. One minister would shout, "Here is Christ," and another minister, "Here and here only is the true Christ." Then the third one, "They are both wrong—here is the only place you will find a true Christ."

Now Joseph had a real problem. Put yourself in his position. Suppose your mother and your sister and a couple of brothers had been proselyted by and had joined the Presbyterian Church. Suppose your father thought that this could not possibly be the true church and was about to join a second group of Christians.

Now here is the crux in Joseph Smith's problem. His mother,

sister, and two brothers had joined one church, and his father was about to join a second. But he, Joseph, though less than fifteen years of age at this time, was a deep thinker and had a mind of his own, and he believed that neither of the two churches in question was the true church. He had been used to hearing the scriptures read almost every day in their home. And so, though he testified that he'd never even approached the eighth grade, after the learning of men, Joseph was quite well educated in the Bible. In the testimony of the Prophet, he was leaning toward a third church and was about to join with a Methodist group.

Then Joseph Smith stopped to think and said, "This just can't be right. They all believe the same Bible apparently, but they don't teach the same things. They interpret the same passages so differently from one another as church groups that I can't see any possibility of their getting together." So he said, "What's to be done? Which is the right church? Which church should I join?" And then he testified that he was reading in the writings of James, and a certain passage so impressed him that the words seemed to stand right out from the page of the book...

> If any of you lack wisdom, let him ask of God, that giveth to all *men* liberally, and upbraideth not; and it shall be given him.
> But let him ask in faith, nothing wavering. For he that wavereth is like a wave of the sea driven with the wind and tossed.
>
> *James 1:5-6*

"Surely that is my answer," he said. So he went out alone into the woods close by his home to offer a vocal prayer to his Heavenly Father. He asked a very simple question. "Which church shall I join?" And he asked it with perfect faith, believing to his very core that he would receive an answer. Then he testified that a spirit of darkness attacked him. He described it as a power of darkness, and although exceedingly strong even at this youthful age, he wrestled physically with this power and was just about to give up in despair when suddenly a light began to appear over his head, finally becoming greater than the brilliance of the noonday sun. Upon appearance of the light, the spirit of darkness, this power that had hold of him and bound his tongue, left him. He said he saw two personages standing above him in the air in a shaft of brilliant light, one standing slightly behind the other. "Joseph," one of them said, and then pointed to the second personage..."This is My Beloved Son. Hear Him!"

> My object in going to inquire of the Lord was to know which of all the sects was right, that I might know which to join. No sooner, therefore, did I get possession of myself, so as to be able to speak, than I asked the Personages who stood above me in the light, which of all the sects was right—and which I should join.
>
> I was answered that I must join none of them, for they were all wrong; (*This was a rather surprising thing and yet surely, he had thought of that possibility, for he had said to himself before he went into the woods to pray, "Could it be possible that they are all wrong together; that none of them is the true Church of Jesus Christ?"*) and the Personage who addressed me said that all their creeds were an abomination in his sight; that those professors were all corrupt; that: "they draw near to me with their lips, but their hearts are far from me, they teach for doctrines the commandments of men, having a form of godliness, but they deny the power thereof."
>
> *The Pearl of Great Price, Joseph Smith 2:18-19*

And Joseph Smith was told many other things including how this drifting away from the true faith took place gradually, until the falling away was finally so complete that Christ himself wouldn't recognize the conglomerate teachings of the many Christian religions, all claiming to believe the Bible, yet none of which taught identically the same doctrines.

Now the boy Prophet had his answer, and the statement came to him, you recall, that if he were faithful, he would be the instrument in the hands of God in restoring the true gospel to the earth.

Following this unparalleled experience, the young man waited for over three years for further divine instruction, and it seemed like an eternity to the Prophet Joseph Smith. Possibly mankind has forgotten the ratio of time with man as against time with God. Remember, one day with God is the time of one rotation of Kolob (the closest planet to the habitation of God) on its axis, which is equal to one thousand years in the timing of men. I took the trouble to break this down mathematically once and found that one of our years is equal to roughly a minute and a half with God. So God had kept Joseph Smith waiting three times one and a half, or less than five minutes, and yet to this young man it seemed like an eternity.

The first vision, you recall, took place in the spring of 1820, so on the 21st of September, 1823, with real anxiousness, Joseph Smith went to his bedroom, and there he prayed with all the fervor in him to see whether there was something wrong with him that he had heard no more from heaven. The he received a marvelous manifestation. A personage appeared to him, again in a shaft of brilliant light* that came through the ceiling of his bedroom.

Note the personal testimony of Joseph Smith and the descriptive detail in his testimony. If you ever get into legal trouble, you just hope and pray that you have witnesses on your side as good as this young man was. Joseph the Prophet never changed his story. Through thick and thin he continued to maintain these things, marvelous things, yet in a straightforward, simple manner,

> ...I discovered a light appearing in my room, which continued to increase until the room was lighter than at noonday, when immediately a personage appeared at my bedside, standing in the air, for his feet did not touch the floor.

---

* I wish I were about fifty years younger and could start out studying this business of the brilliant shaft of light as a possible means of travel and as a possible means of securing power. Later revelations to Joseph Smith, you remember, told him that the very power of God was based on daylight - yes, that light that is reflected from God, from planet to planet to planet, finally to our sun, and then to the earth. Every time these messengers appeared to him, apparently, they appeared either in these shafts of white light brilliant beyond the brightness of the noonday sun, or in a cloud of brilliant white light.

He had on a loose robe of the most exquisite whiteness. It was a whiteness beyond anything earthly I had ever seen; nor do I believe that any earthly thing could be made to appear so exceedingly white and brilliant. His hands were naked, and his arms also, a little above the wrist; so, also, were his feet naked, as were his legs, a little above the ankles. His head and neck were also bare. I could discover that he had no other clothing on but this robe, as it was open, so that I could see into his bosom.

Not only was his robe exceedingly white, but his whole person was glorious beyond description, and his countenance truly like lightning. The room was exceedingly light, but not so very bright as immediately around his person. When I first looked upon him, I was afraid; but the fear soon left me.

He called me by name, and said unto me that he was a messenger sent from the presence of God to me, and that his name was Moroni; that God had a work for me to do; and that my name should be had for good and evil among all nations, kindreds, and tongues, or that it should be both good and evil spoken of among all people.

He said there was a book deposited, written upon gold plates, giving an account of the former inhabitants of this continent, and the source from whence they sprang. He also said that the fullness *(now this is important)* of the everlasting Gospel was contained in it, as delivered by the Savior to the ancient inhabitants *(of this, the American continent);*

The Pearl of Great Price, Joseph Smith 2:30-34

Many other important instructions were given Joseph Smith at this time. Three times during this night of September 21, 1823, this same vision burst upon him. Each time the identical words, which were used in the first session, were given, but in the second and third sessions, additional instructions were given. Joseph testifies that as the third vision ended he looked out of his window, and it was becoming daylight, so the visions had taken the entire night of the 21st of September, 1823.

When he went to work in the fields the next morning, his father noticed he was pale and apparently not feeling well. He said to him, "Joseph, go back to the house and rest awhile, and when you feel better, come back."

Joseph left with the intent to go home, but when he attempted to cross the fence to leave the field, he fell helpless to the ground. At this time, in broad daylight, and for the fourth time now, the Angel Moroni visited him. He repeated everything given to him in the first session the night before. God has long since learned the lesson of repetition. By now Joseph Smith could almost repeat verbatim the words of the Angel Moroni, the message of God to him.

Additional instructions were given in this fourth vision. He was to go to the hill that he had seen in his vision, and there he was to go to the particular spot, which he also had seen in that vision. This is rather amazing. He did go, immediately recognized the hill from his vision, and walked right to the spot that he had particularly seen in the vision. He tells how he was impressed to dig around what appeared to be a boulder. He found that what had been originally a boulder had been cut by someone so that now it was flat on the bottom, rounded on the top and came to sharp edges all the way around the outside. He tried to lift it but couldn't. With the help of a lever he found close by, he raised this stone and found it formed the lid of a stone box. Again note the descriptive detail: Two long stones formed the sides; two shorter ones were on the ends; a long stone formed the bottom, and the stones were cemented together by some sort of mortar. In the bottom of the box, laying crossways were two other stones upon which were placed the golden records and the Urim and Thummim and other things. Joseph reached down to get the plates, but immediately, the Angel Moroni appeared. He told the young prophet that the time for bringing these records forth had not yet arrived. Moroni told Joseph to come to that hill and meet him on the 22nd of September each of the next four years. Joseph testifies that he did this, and each year he received more help from the angel.

We are talking about the "educated man" in this 1964 leadership week of Brigham Young University. Here is the case of a man who was not educated as to the things of the world but who was perhaps the best-educated man as to the things of God ever to live in his day; he was taught and tutored by angels and many messengers of God.

Now let's refer to Joseph Smith's key on the chart of page 4. At the top of the chart, under the caption "KEY" are the numbers (3) (4) (3). The first vision was in 1820. Three years later, 1823, the second group of vision. Then followed the four annual visits to the hill. Finally, on the 22nd day of September 1827, the Prophet Joseph received custody of the plates with a restrictive charge. Then three years later he published the *Book of Mormon*. He was told that if he let those plates get out of his keeping, he would forfeit his very life as a penalty. He was further instructed that he was to show the records to no man except those to whom God would direct him, and that if he did, he would receive a drastic penalty.

The prophet said, "I didn't know what persecution was before I received the plates. I thought I had been persecuted." His neighbors, who didn't believe his story of the vision of God the Father and the Son, Jesus Christ, made fun of him; all over his neighborhood he was being put to shame by those who thought they were in the right. Joseph testifies that he felt very much like Paul in his defense before Agrippa.

> So it was with me. I had actually seen a light, and in the midst of that light I saw two Personages, and they did in reality speak to me; and though I was hated and persecuted for saying that I had seen a vision, yet it was true; and while they were persecuting me, reviling me, and speaking all manner of evil against me falsely for so saying, I was led to say in my heart: Thy persecute me for telling the truth? I have actually seen a vision; and who am I that I can withstand God, or why does the world think to make me deny what I have actually seen? For I had seen a vision; I knew it, and I knew that God knew it, and I could not deny it, neither dared I do it...
>
> *The Pearl of Great Price, Joseph Smith 2:25*

That is quite a testimony regarding the first vision. With the same fervor he continued to maintain that he had seen the Angel Moroni and on many visits had received much instruction from him.

How much did this young man believe these things? He could not even stay at home because of the persecution of his neighbors. He was beaten by mobs and tarred and feathered. All in the world he had to do to stop the persecution was to say. "I deny that I ever saw God the Father and any angels and messengers from heaven who had messages for all the children of the earth." That is all he had to do.

He is a pretty good witness. Worlds without end, they'll never break his testimony down, for he **did** see, and he **did** hear those things, which he said he saw and heard.

Let us follow Joseph Smith to the end of his days. Three years (in round figures) after receiving the plates, he caused that the translation of these ancient golden records, translated by the gift and power of God, be printed in English for the first time as the *Book of Mormon*.

The Prophet became a leader of a great people. He was the founder of the beautiful city of Nauvoo, made out of a swamp area; it became one of the most beautiful cities west of the East Coast of these United States. He was a mayor. He was a general in the armed forces. At the very moment he was murdered in cold blood, he was running for the presidency of these United States. Did you know that? He did not apparently want to run for the presidency, but his friends urged him to do so. And he had a very good chance of getting the presidency, for he had a very wonderful platform. It made good sense even to the people who were prejudiced against him.

Could he have saved his life? Yes, he could. He had escaped his persecutors, had crossed the Mississippi River, and was on his way westward. They his own friends, the only ones who knew his whereabouts, came to him. They said, "Joseph, we think it will be a little easier on the Saints if you will come back just once more—just once, and stand trial." I can almost hear the Prophet's words.

"I have been standing trial time and time again. Every time I have been in court, they have released me without a vestige of evidence against me. Now you are asking me to come back again, and I tell you if I come back again I will never return alive." He knew that. Still his friends insisted, and Joseph said finally. "If my life is of no worth to my friends, it is of no worth to me."

He went back, and as he walked out of that beautiful city of Nauvoo, he said to those around him and his guards, "I am going like a lamb to the slaughter, but I am as calm as a summer's morning. I have a conscience void of offense toward God and toward all men. If they take my life, I shall die an innocent man, and my blood shall cry from the ground for vengeance, and it shall be said of me. 'He was murdered in cold blood.' "

And so he did go to stand trial, with the absolute guarantee of the great state of Illinois, under the hand of its governor, that he would be given the protection of the militia of that state. Yet the facts show that some of that very militia were in the band of painted-faced individuals who murdered him in cold blood while he was supposedly under the protection of the law in Carthage Jail, Illinois, where he was awaiting trial. Yes, he is a marvelous witness for the authenticity of the work, and his testimony will never be broken down. Like many prophets before him, he has sealed his testimony with his blood.

Thank you Clair for acting as proxy for our "Key Witness." You may step down now. Could I get Bud Draper to come forward and act as proxy witness for Oliver Cowdery?

We are taking quite a bit of time on the first two witnesses. The others go much more rapidly, but we will get the gist of this thing from these two witnesses.

Oliver was short and dark and in many physical ways the diametrical opposite of Joseph Smith, who was tall and strapping and rather blond. But Oliver was also different in another way. Where Joseph Smith had only been to school a few days of a few years of his life, never even approaching the eighth grade, Oliver testifies that he had been very well educated. He was a school teacher in the area of Joseph Smith's home when he first heard the "Joe Smith" story and of his "Gold Bible," as it was known then.

Oliver Cowdery testifies that he was born in the year of 1806, a few months after the Prophet. As a young man he went to live with the Smith family, as it was the custom for the teachers of local schools to go board and room with local families as part of their pay. Teachers must not have been paid very well then, because when this fellow went to meet the Prophet Joseph Smith, who had gone down into Pennsylvania, he had to walk most of the way, because he didn't have enough money to pay his way.

How did this young, well-educated individual testify? He said that when he heard the story of Joseph Smith and his "Golden Bible" coming from the lips of Joseph's own parents, he said to himself, "Surely these people believe this story." In spite of all the derogatory things that he had heard in the neighborhood, he testifies, "I was deeply impressed to go meet the Prophet. I had always prided myself in the ability to make rapid decisions upon meeting people as to what type of people they were and whether or not they were honest and trustworthy. I felt sure that if I could meet the Prophet Joseph Smith and talk to him for a short time, I could tell whether he was telling the truth or not."

At his first opportunity, Oliver took a short leave of absence and walked, as I said, most of the way to Pennsylvania to meet the Prophet Joseph Smith, and a strange thing happened. He had been talking with this uneducated farmer boy—uneducated as to the things of men but keenly educated as to the things of God—for only a very few minutes, when the testimony came to him that Joseph Smith was a prophet and that he was telling the truth. And so Oliver said to the Prophet, after a **very short** conversation, "Joseph, I am going to resign my position and come down to help you in the translation of the *Book of Mormon*." Two days after he met the Prophet, Oliver actually started as scribe in the translation of the "golden record."

Now the uneducated boy (after the things of men) had completely convinced the educated young man and the prosecution made note of this. They found it had happened in other cases. Later they told us that Joseph Smith had these men under a spell of some kind, that he must have had a dynamic personality and was able to influence these men beyond all realms of reason.

That was not the reason, as we will see later in the testimony. The reason was that Joseph was telling the truth! Oliver said that nobody could hear Joseph give his testimony and see the truth shining from his eyes without being swayed as to its truthfulness. He further testified, "I watched time and time again as Joseph went in before judges and justices of the peace and juries, in some cases known to be antagonistic toward the Prophet and his work." Remember, this was a young man speaking who later became one of the most renowned attorneys in the Midwest. And he said, "I have watched it happen time and time again. When they heard the story from the lips of the Prophet himself, they believed the story and turned him loose. No charge they could place against him would hold up." Oliver testifies regarding some of these cases, the same as the Prophet did. Regardless of what the trumped-up charge was to begin with (any excuse to get the Prophet and others into court who had part in bringing forth the *Book of Mormon*), sooner or later the examining and the cross-examining evaded the original charge and came around to whether or not the accused were parties to a fraud in bringing forth the *Book of Mormon*. The prosecution and the courts could not place evidence against them that would stand up in a court of law, for there **was no evidence** against them.

Let us follow the life of this young man, Oliver Cowdery. You see on the chart (page 4) beginning in 1829, the year he first met the Prophet, and for nine years thereafter, he was very active in the Church and was with the Prophet on several occasions when supernatural things occurred. Then in the year 1838, he told us in later testimony, the spirit of Satan himself seemed to get into his heart, and after seven out of nine charges were sustained against him in a court of the Church, he was excommunicated, publicly humiliated and cast aside. For ten years he remained out of the Church, some of this time very bitter toward Joseph Smith personally. Yet he had testified that during the nine years he worked very closely with the Prophet in the bringing forth of the *Book of Mormon* and the organization of The Church of Jesus Christ of Latter-day Saints; they became closer than blood brothers. He said "Why, we were as close as two peas in a pod." How dared Joseph Smith antagonize, publicly humiliate and cast aside his closest worker in crime, if such this be? If this be fraud, then these men are criminals and if they are fraudulent criminals, they deserve the worst penalty that man can devise or God can devise, for hundreds of thousands of people have left their homes with all that they hold near and dear and followed the teachings of these men. Many of these people have given their very lives, some out on the plains going west; some, coming across the waters from the old countries; some, in the lands of their birth, in foreign countries; others, after they came into the Church fold. And they gladly gave their lives, if need be, to the cause, because so great was their faith in the teachings of these men. And yet they tell me they are criminals, that they are fraudulent men. And I say, "How dare the arch criminal, if such he were, antagonize his closest worker in this work?"

But when Joseph met with a request to acquiesce in the excommunication of Oliver Cowdery, he didn't hesitate for a second. He said, "If Oliver, of all people, can't live the teachings of the gospel in their fullness, surely we should excommunicate him." And he did not hesitate.

When Oliver Cowdery saw the outrageous things that went on in the name of legal practice after the martyrdom of the Prophet Joseph Smith and his brother, Hyrum, he could resist no longer. Finally he wrote a letter to the high council of the Church, pleading with them to let him go, at his own expense, back to the President of the United States and plead the case of Joseph Smith and bring the murderers to trial in a court that was just and fair.

When I think of what went on "legally" in that so called trial of the murderers of Joseph Smith and his brother Hyrum, the Patriarch of the Church...I was going to say, "it makes my hair stand on end." I used to have enough hair to stand on end, but I don't anymore. Did you know that a grand jury had indicted those murderers and that upon the motion of the indicted men themselves, the trial jury which had been agreed upon by both the prosecution and the defense—the twelve men, "good and true," was disbanded and one lone man was put in its place who was not even a judge? This lone man was later shown to be a member of the very mob which murdered Joseph Smith.

Oliver Cowdery, by now a brilliant lawyer, would of course, be incensed at such proceedings.

Olive Cowdery left another great and vital testimony. He said he and the Prophet read in the translation of the *Book of Mormon* (see *2 Nephi 27:12*, as well as other places) the statement that when that book should come forth in the latter days in its translated form, three special witnesses would testify of its authenticity.

> ...three witnesses shall behold it, by the power of God, besides him to whom the book shall be delivered; and they shall testify to the truth of the book and the things therein.
> And there is none other which shall view it, save it be a few according to the will of God...
>
> *2 Nephi 27:12-13*

It is strange that there were exactly "a few, that is eight," more men who testified that they saw these records. You remember that the *New Testament* tells us the story of how Jesus went to the spirit world and preached to the spirits in prison, and we were told that there were "...a few, that is eight..." that had been saved by water in the time of the flood. (*1 Peter 3:20*) It is interesting, just as a side note, that there were just a "few" more, other than the three special witnesses and one key witness.

When Joseph and Oliver read this in the translation, Oliver said, "I would like to be one of those special witnesses. Do you think I could?" Joseph gave the answer that he always gave when he was in doubt. "There is one sure way to find out. We will ask God." He had that kind of confidence. The Lord answered back that he was to take Oliver, David Whitmer, and Martin Harris and go with them into the woods. If it so be that they were faithful they might be the special witnesses. Oliver testifies that they went into the woods and that they did receive a marvelous manifestation, but that a peculiar thing happened first.

They had agreed to pray in a circle one at a time. As I recall, they had finished praying twice around and were about to start the third round when Martin Harris, according to Oliver's testimony and Martin's testimony, said to the Prophet Joseph Smith, "I am sorry, Joseph, I am the reason you aren't receiving an answer, I just don't have faith enough." And he asked for permission to withdraw into another part of the forest. (We will take up the sequel of Martin Harris after recess.) He did. And then, on the very next prayer, Oliver said a marvelous manifestation broke upon them, and as a result of that manifestation he and others signed the testimony, which has been in the forepart of the *Book of Mormon* for many years.

> BE IT KNOWN unto all nations, kindreds, tongues, and people, unto whom this work shall come: That we, through the grace of God the Father, and our Lord Jesus Christ, have seen the plates which contain this record, which is a record of the people of Nephi, and also of the Lamanites, their brethren, and also of the people of Jared, who came from the tower of which hath been spoken. **And we also know that they have been translated by the gift and power of God, for HIS voice hath declared it unto us;** wherefore we know of a surety that the work is true. And we also testify that we have seen the engravings which are upon the plates; and they have been shown unto us by the power of God, and not of man. *(Now note this carefully, in case you haven't read this*

recently.) And we declare with words of soberness, that an angel of God came down from heaven, and he brought and laid before our eyes, that we beheld and saw the plates, and the engravings thereon; and we know that it is by the grace of God the Father, and our Lord Jesus Christ, that we beheld and bear record that these things are true. And it is marvelous in our eyes. Nevertheless, **the voice of the Lord commanded us that we should bear record of it; wherefore, to be obedient unto the commandments of God, we bear testimony of these things.** And we know that if we are faithful in Christ, we shall rid our garments of the blood of all men, and be found spotless before the judgment-seat of Christ, and shall dwell with him eternally in the heavens. And the honor be to the Father, and to the Son, and to the Holy Ghost, which is one God. Amen.

> *OLVER COWDERY*
> *DAVID WHITMER*
> *MARIN HARRIS*

You remember, we were talking about the testimony of Oliver Cowdery. Oliver had testified that he wanted to be one of the three special witnesses. He went into the woods to pray with Joseph Smith and the others and did become one of the three special witnesses to the authenticity of the *Book of Mormon*.

One day, long after Oliver's excommunication, a fellow attorney met Oliver on the street. He had in his hand a *Book of Mormon*, opened to the page where the testimony of the three witnesses was recorded. "I see your name attached to this book as one of its special witnesses." Let's get the actual trial testimony of this incident. The prosecution, by the way, brought out this conversation between Oliver and his attorney friend.

Someone asked me a moment ago if the prosecution was able to say anything against the book. In nearly three weeks of the mock trial I heard things I didn't have the least idea existed! I didn't realize when I got into this mock trial like a "babe in the woods" that there had been over 1,500 books written as commentaries upon the *Book of Mormon*! Did you know that? And many of those 1,500 books have been written specifically **against** the *Book of Mormon*.

So the prosecution brought into court things I had never heard of, things which **seemed** to be very fine evidence against the record. But as we got down to the facts of the matter, down to the core of the truth, we found that many times things which seemed to be against the record in testimony boomeranged. They were like that little thing from that land "way down under," that trails way out some place and seems to be getting somewhere and then turns clear around until it hits the thrower right in the back of the neck with the "evidences" they brought into court. Time after time they wished they had never mentioned a particular point. Now we have a case in point here: Remember, the opposing attorneys brought this previously mentioned conversation between Oliver Cowdery and his lawyer friend into court as evidence that Oliver had denied his testimony.

The question: "Mr. Cowdery, I see your name attached to this book (the *Book of Mormon*) as one of its special witnesses. Do you believe this book?"

And the answer:

"No, sir."

Well that hit me like a bolt out of the blue. I thought I had thoroughly searched the life of Oliver Cowdery, and I had found no evidence anywhere of his having denied his testimony. And yet here appeared to be a denial in Oliver's conversation with his attorney friend.

When we got into the record from which the prosecution had given this quote, I became very curious. And I found, lo and behold, that the one who wrote this denial, in the book they were quoting from, was not the person who was having the conversation with Oliver Cowdery, nor was he present on the occasion. Therefore, it was hearsay, and it would not stand up as evidence in a court of law. Now I was still curious and thought there must be some basis for the story. So I searched in the writings of Oliver

Cowdery, and found that he had mentioned this very episode. I then found a letter, written by the other man who was a party to the conversation. He had mentioned it in a letter to a friend.

When we got the **full** answer, this was what it said: (Notice the nicety of wording of an attorney.) "I see your name attached to this book (the *Book of Mormon*) as one of its special witnesses. Do you believe this book?" The answer did start out "No, sir," but then it went on to say: "My name is attached to this book, and what I then said is true. I **did** see this, and I **know** I saw it. Belief and faith has nothing to do with it as a perfect knowledge has swallowed up the belief and faith I formerly had in the work, **knowing** as I do that the work is true."

Well, you can see how the prosecuting attorneys wished they had never brought up that point.

Oliver Cowdery asked for readmittance into the Church again in the year 1848, not as a high priest, not as an apostle, in the higher priesthood, but as a deacon in the lower priesthood. He was readmitted to the Church, and thousands upon thousands of people heard his ringing testimony.

Even while he was out of the Church, though somewhat bitter towards the Prophet Joseph Smith for having excommunicated him and publicly humiliating him before his friends and the world, Oliver Cowdery never denied his testimony. Some time after his excommunication he was in a courtroom one day as a practicing attorney. In an effort to defeat Cowdery in his case, a fellow attorney charged, in a derogatory way, that Oliver Cowdery could not be trusted very far because he believed in angels and angelic visitations, as Joseph Smith of the famous "Gold Bible" did. The charge went into the records of the particular case that was on trial, and so Oliver Cowdery stood up, asked that his testimony in turn be put into the records of that law case, and it did get into the records. I have the writings of one who was in that courtroom who was not a member of the Church. This individual said anybody who heard Oliver Cowdery make that beautiful statement in court, and seeing the truth standing out and flashing from his eyes, couldn't possibly believe that he was untruthful. The people were deeply impressed. Oliver Cowdery was very well thought of. In part, this was his answer to the accusation and the testimony written in the court records:

> May it please the court and gentlemen of the jury: My brother attorney on the other side has charged me with connection with Joseph Smith and the "Golden Bible." The responsibility has been placed upon me, and I cannot escape reply. Before God and man I dare not deny what I have said—what my testimony contains, as written and printed on the first page of the *Book of Mormon.* May it please your Honor and gentlemen of the jury, this I say: I saw the angel and heard the voice from heaven. How can I deny it? It happened in the daytime when the sun was shining brightly in the firmament, not at night when I was asleep. The glorious messenger from heaven, dressed in a white robe, standing above the ground in a glory I have never seen anything to compare with, the sun insignificant in comparison, told us if we denied that testimony there is no forgiveness in this life or in the world to come. How can I deny it? I dare not, I **will** not.

No, Oliver Cowdery never denied his testimony. As a matter of fact, when he was about to go meet his Maker, he drew all those near and dear to him around his bed, and with the very last breath he breathed on this earth, he testified to the authenticity of the *Book of Mormon* and that the golden plates did actually exist.

Now, you remember Joseph Smith had been told that when the translation was completed, the Angel Moroni would call for the golden records; approximately two-thirds of the records were sealed and were to come forth at a later time, and the entire record was to be kept safe in the hands of God's messengers to stand as a final witness before the entire world in the last days—to condemn those who had heard the story and who had every reason to believe that it was true, and still, deliberately and with full intent, knowingly decided not to accept the gospel. The final evidence will be the records themselves. Now because the Angel had told Joseph this, many in the world have assumed that there were no golden records and therefore they were never placed on public display.

You remember the endless and extreme trouble Joseph Smith had when he got the plates! He said it seemed that everyone within reach of him was divided into two groups: one, the group that didn't believe he had the records, and so wanted to break into where he was supposed to be hiding them to prove that he didn't have any gold plates. The other group, who did believe he had them, wanted to break in and get them for the monetary value of the gold in them. So the Prophet said it seemed that everybody was against him, except a mere handful, comparatively speaking, who believed the story. Now God had said that he would set up special witnesses and a few others to testify that these records actually existed. And he did.

As I have said, in these mock trials, because of the preponderance of legal talent on the one side, a great advantage accrued to them. Many times, on a technicality, a case was quickly thrown out of court because **many** individuals working as a team had been able to think of something which one of them working alone might have missed. As an example, the very first charge the prosecution made regarding the so-called fraudulent nature of the *Book of Mormon* was that it could not be shown with evidence that would stand up in a court of law in this day and age, that there ever were indeed such ancient golden records as the ones Joseph Smith described. You see, they thought that Joseph Smith was the only one who ever saw those records, and that he only "saw" them as a figment of his imagination. And they believed confidently that they could prove this in court. But, of course, they could not prove it, and they were shocked and amazed when I brought the testimony of twelve individuals, all honest, truthful men, well-thought-of in their home areas—competent witnesses. They had been prime parties to the occurrences, and when their testimonies stood up, the prosecution was amazed and had no foundation in fact for their statement that the ancient records did not indeed exist in this day and age.

Oliver Cowdery's testimony helped establish the fact of the existence of the gold plates and the authenticity of the work. We can now let the proxy witness step down.

We next called a proxy witness to represent David Whitmer on the stand. David was the wealthy son of a very well-to-do farming family in the area where Joseph Smith lived. According to his testimony, he was born in the same year as Joseph Smith, in the year 1805.

He testified that he was a personal friend of Oliver Cowdery. When Oliver decided to go down into Pennsylvania from western New York State to meet the Prophet to see if he could tell from a personal visit whether he was honest or not, David asked Oliver to write him a letter, telling him what he thought of the Prophet.

"I got the letter all right from Oliver Cowdery," David testified, "and it not only told me that he believed that Prophet to be a true Prophet, but he also asked me to come down there quickly because he couldn't wait until I met him."

David Whitmer was very well educated. His visit with the Prophet Joseph was the second time a very well educated young man, as to learning of men, had talked with the poor farmer boy who had never even approached the eighth grade in the learning of men. In a very short time, David too, became so convinced that Joseph was telling the truth that he was willing to drop everything he had to follow this Prophet of God in this day and age. He lived to see the day when his family became very active members of the Church. As we follow his story from the beginning as charted on page 4, he first met the Prophet Joseph Smith in 1829. For nine years David was very active in the Church. What did he testify to? His testimony was practically identical to that of Oliver Cowdery as to the angel in the woods, the bringing of the golden records, and his seeing these records as the leaves were turned before his eyes. Now note this: He, as did the others of the special witnesses, testified that he not only saw the records, but he handled them with his own hands. So there could be no possible question of their actual physical existence in the day and age of about 1830.

What happened to David Whitmer after he was active for nine years? He also testified that in his later life it seemed as if the spirit of evil got into his heart. After he wrote a very insulting letter in which he signed himself President of the Church, and after four other charges were sustained against this man in a court of the Church, he, too, was excommunicated, publicly humiliated, and cast aside.

Money matters usually cause dissension between so-called criminals. In crime we have found that every crime has to have a motive, and that some of the motives, which are most potent, are the desire for power, the desire for wealth, and the desire for fame. Power, wealth, and fame are the three basic and prime motivations for crime. We found almost ideal conditions existing among the twelve witnesses (the three special witnesses, the one key witness and the eight other witnesses) for a betrayal of each other, if the *Book of Mormon* had been a fraudulent work. Had there been collusion between the Prophet and the witnesses, they, of necessity, would have had to hold together. A disagreement on the part of any of them would have meant destruction of their entire fraud, if it had been such.

However, the bold action of the Prophet Joseph and of the church when these men deviated is evidence that their work was not fraudulent. There was nothing to fear. And yet the arising dissensions gave every opportunity to expose the work had it been untrue. First, enmity came through the disturbing of possible power on the part of Oliver Cowdery. With David Whitmer matters of wealth entered the picture. When the Law of Consecration came into the Church, Joseph Smith went to David Whitmer, one of the wealthiest men in the Church, and asked him to be one of the first examples in deeding over to the Bishop of the Church with a deed that could not be broken, all of his property, all his wealth. David did not hesitate. That occurred within the nine years that he was very active in the Church. When he was excommunicated from the Church, he neither asked for nor got one penny of that wealth back again.

With the development of such extreme circumstances, certainly Oliver Cowdery or David Whitmer would have exposed Joseph Smith if he had not been a true Prophet of God, and if the *Book of Mormon* had not been the work of God.

David Whitmer is the only one of the three special witnesses who died out of the Church. Yet, as we follow his life after having given his testimony, we find some peculiar things happening. In the very sunset of his life, as he terms it himself, he heard that somebody had said that he had denied his testimony as one of the witnesses to the *Book of Mormon*. Remember, he had signed that statement which Oliver Cowdery had also signed in the forepart of the *Book of Mormon*, as one of the special witnesses.

David became so concerned about this rumor that came to his attention—some man having said that he had denied his testimony, that he went to 19 of the greatest men in his home area where he had lived for over forty years—judges, justices of the peace, bank presidents, publishers and others—nineteen of them and not one of them was a member of The Church of Jesus Christ of Latter-day Saints. He said to these men, "Would you be willing to go under oath and testify to the world that you have known me long and intimately and that my word can be taken the same as my bond?" And they said, "Why certainly we would be willing to do that, David." Then they wanted to know what it was all about. And he said, "I'm not going to answer that question until I have an unqualified answer of yes or no from you gentlemen." Well, their answer was yes; they would give such testimony. And then he said he sprang the trap. He said, "I am going to once and for all testify in print and have it published all around the earth, that

I have never at any time denied my testimony as a witness to the *Book of Mormon*, and I am going to further testify that I have always adhered to that testimony. Then right under that I want your sworn statement that I am honest and dependable." And he said, "I thought sure some of these men would back out when I told them that, but they didn't."

The following is what David Whitmer caused to be published for the first time under the date of March 25, 1881, over fifty years after he had testified to the authenticity of the *Book of Mormon*. It appeared first in the Richmond, Ray County, Conservator of Missouri. Notice how polite David Whitmer was in speaking of the man who had wrongly accused him. He didn't come right out and say, "He's a liar." He just said, "To the end thereof that he may understand me now, if he did not then, and that the world may know the truth..."

Unto all nations, tongues, and people unto whom these presents shall come: It having been represented by one Jacob Murphy of Palo, Caldwell County, Missouri, that I, in conversation with him last summer, denied my testimony as one of the three witnesses to the Book of Mormon; to the end thereof that he may understand me now if he did not then, and that the world may know the truth, I wish now, standing in the very sunset of life and in the fear of God, once and for all to make this public statement: I have never at any time denied that testimony or any part thereof. I have always adhered to that testimony. I do again affirm the truth of all my statements as then made and published. It was no delusion. In the spirit of Christ I submit these statements unto the world, God being my judge as to the sincerity of my motives.

Signed and sealed:

David Whitmer

Immediately following is this statement:

We the undersigned citizens of Richmond, Ray Co., Mo., where David Whitmer Sr. has resided since the year 1838, certify that we have been long and intimately acquainted with him, and know him to be a man of highest integrity and of undoubted truth and veracity. Given at Richmond, Missouri, this March 20th A.D., 1881.

Signed and sealed:

A.W. Doniphan

George W. Dunn (Judge of the Judicial circuit)

T.J. Woodson (Pres. Of the Ray County Savings Bank)

J.T. Child (Editor of the *Conservator*)

And if I had time we would go on down the entire list of the other fifteen.

David Whitmer was not satisfied with having these statements printed in the Richmond, Ray County, papers, so he sent a certified reprint to the *New York Times,* and asked them to print it in the forepart of their newspaper. They did. Then he sent a reprint to the great *London Times.* That paper, together with the *New York Times,* had world-wide circulation. And this declaration and statement was news!

Many captains who had piloted ships all over this world had come into New York Harbor and testified that they had been in many lands where the name of the great President of these United States, Abraham Lincoln, had never been heard, but they had never been in a land where the name of the Prophet Joseph Smith had not been heard and where people did not have some opinion one way or the other, either for or against his work. Anything that had to do with the *Book of Mormon* was news, and so these great newspapers gladly published this article. Just before he died, David asked the *New York Times* to print the story again, this time on the front page, and they did.

As David Whitmer was about to draw his last breath (the only member of the three special witnesses to die out of the Church) he still felt so keenly about his testimony he had given in regard to the coming forth of the *Book of Mormon* and the truthfulness of that book that he brought his family around him, and testified to them that he had never joined another church because he did not believe there was any other true church on the earth. His feelings, as nearly as we can tell, had been hurt. He was not as bitter toward the Prophet as Oliver had been at one period, but he never rejoined the Church. Yet, as he called these greatly loved ones around his bed, he said to them, "I have never denied my testimony; I want you to stand up for me since I won't be here in person to do it, and you tell them that on my deathbed, in the fear of God, my maker, I testified to you to the last breath I drew on this earth that I had never denied my testimony regarding the coming forth of the *Book of Mormon*."

Thus we concluded the testimony of David Whitmer.

Next we called a proxy witness for Martin Harris to the stand. If we had a "doubting Thomas" among the witnesses, I'm afraid Martin Harris would be it. You remember Martin Harris was the one in the forest who said to Joseph Smith and the other witnesses, "I'm sorry, Joseph, but I'm the reason you aren't receiving an answer to your prayer; I just don't have faith enough," and he asked for the privilege of withdrawing to another part of the forest. Then he withdrew to an area of the forest a little distance from the others and knelt down and prayed with all of his heart that he could gain enough faith. He did not **want** to doubt. He said, "I heard a noise behind me, and I turned around and saw the Prophet Joseph Smith coming toward me. I only had to take one look and I knew that they had received a marvelous testimony in answer to their prayer. He told me the story of the angel that came to show the other witnesses the golden plates and then he said that he felt as though a great load had been lifted from his shoulders, for now others had seen and had heard and Oliver Cowdery and David Whitmer knew that there were such things as angels in this day and age and they knew that the golden records existed.*

Martin pleaded with Joseph to join him in prayer that he, too, might still be one of the special witnesses. Joseph readily consented, and before they had prayed very long, the identical vision which Joseph Smith, Oliver Cowdery and David Whitmer had seen together, now burst upon the two of them—Joseph Smith and Martin Harris—the same angel from heaven turning the leaves of the same golden records—the same voice out of heaven purporting to be the voice of God testifying to the authenticity of the record and the correctness of the translation.

Martin Harris was overjoyed and cried out: " 'Tis enough; 'tis enough; mine eyes have beheld; mine eyes have beheld!"

Nevertheless, in his extreme caution, Martin Harris very carefully checked with Oliver Cowdery and David Whitmer individually, to make absolutely sure he had seen and heard the same identical vision they had seen and heard and then only did he join with them in the written testimony in the forepart of the *Book of Mormon*.

Martin Harris further testified that he was born in the year 1783, thus being about twenty-two years older than the other witnesses we have discussed. He was a farmer, a very, very thorough farmer. He was not wealthy, but neither was he poor. He was well-esteemed in this area, a very fine neighbor, but he was cautious, He did not jump into things. But he said, "When I heard Joseph Smith tell the story of the first and second great visions, there could be no question in my mind. I knew that he had seen and had heard what he said he saw and heard. As cautious as I was, I knew this." His testimony continued, "I met the Prophet two years before the other witnesses, in 1827; and when I went to

---

* Some people out of the Church have said, "Do you mean to say that Oliver Cowdery was a scribe for the greatest part of the translation of the Book of Mormon, and yet had never seen the golden records?" Oliver testified that when the Prophet was translating he would always sit in another room, and his words would come through the door or over a screen separating the scribe from the translator. Oliver never saw those records until he saw them in the miraculous episode in the forest.

mortgage my farm to help in the publication of the *Book of Mormon*, I lost my happy home over it." His wife must have said to him, "Well, you old fool, if you want to mortgage your half of the farm to help print that fictitious book, that's all right with me, but you aren't going to mortgage my half of the farm." She divorced him, and Martin Harris mortgaged his half of the farm for $3,000 to pay for the publication of the first five thousand copies of the *Book of Mormon*.

Now, some of the leaders in other churches who had been shouting "blasphemy" at all the claims of the Prophet now stood up in their majesty behind their pulpits saying, "We testify, in the name of Jesus Christ, that it yet will become known how foolish Martin Harris was to mortgage his farm for $3,000 to pay for the first five thousand copies of the *Book of Mormon*, when those copies lie on the shelf gathering dust and rot away for lack of sales."

You know that one of the tests of a prophet is that his prophecies shall come true. Those people were not prophets, were they? The first five thousand copies **did** sell, and some fifty-five English editions have sold since then, each one greater in number than the one before. Martin had said time and time again that what appeared to be doubt on his part was not really doubt; he was simply trying to get more help to persuade others. He insisted on getting the translation of the first 116 pages of the *Book of Mormon*. He wanted to take the translated pages home to prove to his wife that the book was not founded on the spirit of Satan but that it was indeed founded on the spirit of Jesus Christ. Well, those 116 pages were lost and there was quite an ado about it in the early history of the Church.

It was also Martin Harris who took certain transcripts of the ancient hieroglyphics, together with the interpretation that Joseph Smith had given, to New York to the greatest Egyptologist or master of ancient languages in the day, Professor Charles Anthon of Columbia University. Having presented this information, Martin testified that he got a certificate from the professor stating that not only were the characters Egyptian in type but also that the translation was the most nearly perfect of any translation of ancient Egyptian he had seen. As Martin Harris went to leave, having this certification in his pocket, the professor asked him where the record came from. He answered that an angel of God had come down from heaven and shown where the records were hidden. The professor, according to the testimony of Martin Harris, asked for the certificate he had written. When it was returned to him, he tore it into shreds saying that there was no such thing now as ministering of angels. (He had not read *Revelation* 14:6-7 very carefully, had he?)

Later, in a meeting of scientists, Professor Anthon verified that he had given Martin Harris a certificate regarding the translation of the ancient script. Then he explained that he had torn it up when he found that the gold plates had been brought by angels, and he smirked and said to the other scientists, "Any of us knows that there are no angels in this day and age."

After his experience with Professor Anthon, Martin Harris took the copy of the characters and the translation of them to Dr. Mitchell, another expert in languages of the ancient people, and he got verification of the same thing that Professor Anthon had told him regarding the correctness of the characters and the interpretation.

Now what happened to Martin Harris after ten years of activity in the Church? The church moved West. He said to the people around him; "I never did leave the Church. The Church left me." Geographically speaking, that was true, for when the Church moved west, he told the brethren that he was getting kind of old and suggested that they go ahead and get things set and he would follow later. He had good intentions, but for thirty-three long years this man was a tiny island of belief in a whole sea of unbelief around him. His neighbors testified in writing and under oath that Martin Harris was just as honest as the day is long and that he was one of the finest neighbors anyone could have. They thought, however, that there was just one subject on which he was "jest a little tetched"—he still continued to maintain that he saw an angel of God and the golden records from which he claimed Joseph Smith translated the *Book of Mormon*. And he testified that God himself spoke from the heavens to him and told him that the translation was authentic and divine.

In the sunset of this man's life some of the Saints in the Rocky Mountains raised a fund and sent it to him, and he went out to the West. There hundreds and thousands of people heard his sweet testimony regarding his part in bringing forth the *Book of Mormon* and relating to the actuality of the existence of the ancient golden records.

And a third time it happened—three out of three! As he was about to go meet his Maker and was drawing his last breath on this earth, he called those near and dear to him around his deathbed, and he died with a testimony of the *Book of Mormon* on his lips.

Thus, all of the "Three Witnesses" avowed the truth of the *Book of Mormon* in their dying breaths. And therefore, we conclude the testimony of Martin Harris.

By now the prosecuting attorneys were virulent, "We refuse to accept the testimonies of angelic visitations. We refuse to accept the testimony of God's voice out of heaven! We don't even think those things exist!"

And I continued to say to them as sweetly as I could, with a smile on my face, "I am not asking you to accept anything super-natural, if you can't accept. All I am asking you to do is to accept the testimony of competent **human** witnesses who were there when these things happened, who were honest men, who were not fraudulent in nature and who continued to maintain the testi-monies to their deathbeds that they did see and hear the things they said they saw and heard. And that testimony you **cannot** refuse to accept in any court of law in this land."

The judge continued to rule in support of fact. The prosecution had to accept it because it was the testimony of human witnesses, even though that testimony brought in supernatural occurrences. I said, "Would you feel better if I were to bring you the testimony of eight men of various ages, backgrounds, livelihoods, some who died in the Church, some who died out of the Church, some who apostatized, some who were excommunicated—eight men who disagreed on many things later in their lives, but who continued to maintain one thing in common to their deathbeds? Would you feel better if I could bring you the testimonies of eight such men, testifying that in broad daylight Joseph Smith showed them the golden records—that they handled and hefted them—no voices out of heaven—no supernatural occurrences?" They didn't think we could do it, but said, "It would help us a lot."

Then I called the "Eight Witnesses" by proxy to the stand, one by one. I introduced Christian Whitmer, then Jacob Whitmer, Peter Whitmer, Jr., and John Whitmer.

The prosecution began to protest and said, "Well, of course, if you are going to stay in one family, naturally they will stay together in their testimony."

So we began to bring in a couple of test cases here. We found that it was anything but natural for any family, as a group, to see something and later on agree as to what they had seen and heard.

"If it will make you happier, I will call another witness." So we called Hiram Page, sort of a lone wolf, and then followed Joseph Smith Sr., the father of the Prophet; then Hyrum Smith, who was right alongside the Prophet as a martyr to the cause. Finally, last but not least, the first great missionary of the Church, Samuel H. Smith, a brother of the Prophet.

There are the eight men and what did they testify to? It is in print for the world to read, and has been for over a hundred years, in the forepart of the *Book of Mormon*. Note the complete absence, if you please, of anything supernatural.

BE IT KNOWN unto all nations, kindreds, tongues, and people, unto whom this work shall come: That Joseph Smith, Jun., the translator of this work, has shown unto us the plates of which hath been spoken, which have the appearance of gold; and as many of the leaves as the said Smith has translated we did handle with our hands; and we also saw the engravings thereon, all of which has the appearance of ancient work, and of curious workmanship. And this we bear record with words of soberness, that the said Smith has shown unto us, for we have seen and hefted, and know of a surety that the said Smith has got the plates of which we have spoken. And we give our names unto the world, to witness unto the world that which we have seen. And we lie not, God bearing witness of it.

CHRISTIAN WHITMER   HIRAM PAGE
JACOB WHITMER   JOSEPH SMITH, SEN.
PETER WHITMER, JUN.   HYRUM SMITH
JOHN WHITMER   SAMUEL H. SMITH

In broad daylight, as one man would hand something tangible to a group of men, Joseph Smith handed the records to these eight men. They handled them, turned the pages with their own fingers, and they knew positively that the golden plates existed.

As a climax to the testimonies, I called upon the key witness, the Three Witnesses and the Eight Witnesses to stand in a body. Then I addressed the court, "Here are twelve witnesses, all of whom have testified that they saw and handled the ancient golden records from which the *Book of Mormon* was translated."

Did these witnesses have ulterior motives in giving their testimonies? One of four things could be true:

First. These men actually could be **imposters** deliberately deceiving the public, **perpetrating a fraud** with the intent to deceive. Now if this were the case, there must be a **motive.** Could it be **fame?** That is a ridiculous proposition. If anyone of these men wanted to become world famous, all he had to do was turn "state's evidence," and his name would have been emblazoned over the greatest newspapers in the world. No, the motive was not fame. Was it **power?** Now there is a strange thing. Even though some of these men sat on the council which selected the second-ranking group in authority in the Church—the Council of the Twelve Apostles—not one of these men was a member of the Council of the Twelve Apostles, the body second in authority to the First Presidency. Not one of these men was a counselor in the First Presidency of the Church when it was organized, the first body in authority. Now had these men been after power as a motive for fraud, surely they would have asked for and received the highest positions in the Church in payment for their perfidy. Power was not the motive, then. Was it wealth? Positively not, when we get all the facts. Here was Martin Harris, giving, giving and not getting! Here was David Whitmer, giving all his fortune and not getting it back when he was excommunicated. No, if wealth were the motive, they did not fulfill their motive, and they certainly would have exposed the fraud. The facts showed that no motives of any kind existed for fraud.

Second. Were these men **enthusiasts?** Were they so built up with enthusiasm that they thought they saw and heard things they did not see and hear? Maybe, but the facts of this particular case won't bear it out. How long will enthusiasm stay at that white-hot heat—through excommunication, through apostasy, through bitterness? No, no! Their enthusiasm would have cooled long, long before their deathbeds, but they still continued to maintain these things to their deathbeds.

Third. Were they **deluded?** Remember the testimony of the only one of the three special witnesses who died out of the Church? **"It was no delusion."** Well, did Joseph Smith, indeed, have a power over these men as the prosecution thought he did? If he did, then they must give him supernatural powers, which they were not willing to do, for he continued to maintain that power, if that were the point, long after he was dead and in the grave.

Fourth. Were they **truthful** men? Yes! The fourth element is the only one of four possibilities which will stand up. What they testified to was **true!** The record is true. The way of its coming forth is true! It will stand throughout the ages as the only possible answer to the existence of the great *Stick of Joseph.*

Do not sell the *Book of Mormon* short, brothers and sisters! You have a testimony in your hearts; I am sure of it. I humbly pray that that testimony may grow and grow into a living fire, and if there are those with us who do not have a testimony, I humbly pray that you will get a testimony of this great work and be able to carry it on to others in the earth.

Prologue to
ACT II

YOU NOTICE we have a whole group of charges here (see page 48) which the prosecution made against the Book of Mormon and those who brought it forth. Had any one of these charges been sustained by fact, our case would have been greatly weakened, but we found not one of these statements to be true. In many cases just the opposite was true.

First, they charged that the Bible was the whole word of God; and that therefore the heavens were closed. You missionaries who have been in the field have heard that many times.

Second, they charged that another Bible was not needed. The facts did not bear this out.

Third, they charged that the *Book of Mormon* could not be true because it contradicted the *Bible*. We found that this statement was not true.

Fourth, they charged that the *Book of Mormon* was a fiction story, first stating that it was written by Joseph Smith, then by a whole group of modern-day people. We found that that was not true and that it was not a fiction story.

Fifth, (the prosecution was beginning to grab for straws now, going down for the second time,) they said that if the book was true, it would not make so many ridiculous statements. We have to admit that in the year 1830, many statements in the book sounded fantastic beyond belief, but you will see how we answered that charge to the court's complete satisfaction.

Sixth, they said (and this time they were going down for the third time,) that if the book were true, it would be more popular. I began to ask what popularity and truth necessarily had to do with each other. Many times, because a thing is true, it is unpopular. Jesus Christ's teachings were very unpopular with many people to the point that they crucified him. But that fact certainly didn't make his teachings untrue, did it?

In this second session or second lecture on *The Trial of the Stick of Joseph*, we will go almost completely to the words and pages of the *Stick of Joseph* itself, letting it answer these charges for and of itself. We will find the answers are beautiful, that the answers are authentic, that the answers are conclusive, that it will stand on its own feet, and that it is its own best witness, after all.

Our theme in this 1954 leadership week is "Who is the Educated Man?" We have discussed the education of several of the personal witnesses in the first lecture. Let me give you just a little background of my education while simultaneously giving more background on *The Trial of the Stick of Joseph*. I was born and raised in Salt Lake City and attended Wasatch School and Bryant Junior High School. There my formal schooling ended.

After three doctors had told Dad and Mother that I could not live more than a few months because of a heart condition, Mother and three of my sisters took me to California in 1921 to **die**— because it was a pretty place to "push up daisies." A serious siege of rheumatic fever had left me with enlargement of the heart and two leaking valves.

We had only been in California a few months when Dad was sent down on a stretcher with a stroke—not expected to live. It looked like the Lord wanted us in California. Since I was the only boy in a family of eight, (Dad, Mother, five sisters and myself) I didn't have time to die. I had to get busy and help make a living. No one would hire me because of my heart condition, so I started the May-Bell Dairy in Maywood and Bell, near Los Angeles. I solicited all day long the first day and came home with a one-quart customer, as tickled as a kid with a new toy. We did very well. From this standing start, in ten months we had four retail routes and three wholesale routes, with Dad lying in bed keeping the books, the girls filling the milk bottles and my cousins milking the cows. We sold-out in ten months time for enough so that Dad and I could go into the mortgage loan and building business together. (He was by now up in a wheelchair.) The Lord was real good to us and we prospered.

But, even though I was working full time, I had a driving desire for an education. It was rough, but I am sure we appreciate something more when we have to fight for it than if it is handed to us on a platter. I wasn't just after fun and a sheepskin, I was after an education. Los Angeles Evening High School became home base for a minimum of three nights a week, then Los Angeles Adult Evening School, and then private tutoring, extension courses, part-time classes, and correspondence courses and my education began to round out. If LaSalle Correspondence School knew what we did with their courses they would send some more of us a bill. We used to pass the material from fellow to fellow until he had worn it to a frazzle. I attended part-time classes at U.C.L.A. when they were still on Vermont Street before they moved to Westwood, and so it went, my education picture gradually filling in. After college I went on through the equivalent of four years of law and all the while I was getting perhaps the best education of all in the "School of Hard Knocks."

Dad and I both lost sizeable fortunes in the financial crash of 1929. Part of the time during the depression, I was working for Golden State Dairies in Long Beach. They would look at you like you had stolen the company safe if you put in less than 14 hours a day and then I was trying to study law on the side, and of course, it was a problem. It was during this period that the "mock trial" took place in an extension course in the Long Beach Adult Evening School out in East Long Beach just after the Long Beach earthquake in 1932.

I didn't take legal training, ever, with the idea of practicing law. I had always felt that with my red hair and Irish background I could get into plenty of trouble on my own without borrowing trouble from others as an attorney. Father and I, as I have said, had been in the mortgage loan business and construction business together and it seemed that we were spending half our time in court. We both felt that legal training would be very helpful in our business as a "preventive measure"—you know, "an ounce of prevention is worth a pound of cure"—and since I was a "couple of days" younger than Dad, I was elected to go back to school.

All I had intended to do was to take some business law, but I became so fascinated with the whole field of law, that I completed the equivalent of a four-year course in about nine years of a class here and a class there. It has been extremely helpful in our business, which is in its thirty-third year and third generation. I wouldn't trade anything for that legal training. And I'm happy to report that we've spent very little time in court since then. We have learned to be extra careful to have a good understanding to begin with and then if trouble does arise to follow Jesus Christ's amonition: "Agree with thine adversary quickly, whiles thou art in the way with him..." In other words, settle out of court—don't fight. (*See Matthew 5:25, 26, 39-41.*)

We don't make conversions with argumentation and by fighting. It took me years to learn that. We make them with love and prayer, with humble testimony, with kindness and with a spirit of friendliness, - never with animosity and trying to show that someone else is wrong.

I'm sorry I didn't have the missionary spirit during the mock trial that I later acquired. I was not so interested in making friends as I was in winning a lawsuit and I'm afraid I rode roughshod over those young "budding" attorneys of the prosecution more than once. But I want to tell you this: Although I was the only member of the Church in the class where this mock trial was held and although there was some bitterness on the part of the opposition, particularly when they kept getting hit with their own boomerang—you see their charges kept coming back and hitting them in the back of the neck, - yet they were deeply impressed with the testimony given.

It appears that the facts, as brought out in *The Trial of the Stick of Joseph,* are helpful to some people in building a stronger testimony of the truth of the *Book of Mormon* and if they help even one in an audience, I'm certainly happy to spend any time required in giving the lectures and in giving this information to the world.

ACT II
Defense by INTERNAL EVIDENCE
(Compare Ezekiel 37:15-19 with 1 Nephi 13:38, 41 and Mormon 7:8-9)

CHARGES	REFERENCES	ANSWERS
1. Bible is whole word of God – heavens closed	Rev. 22:18 Deut. 4:2 1 Nephi 13:24, 26, 29 Exo. 24:7; Num 21:14; Josh. 10:13; 1 Chr. 29:29; 1 Cor. 5:9	No Bible when Rev. written. God has never said that He would not add to his words. Bible not complete —parts missing.
2. Another Bible not needed	Ezek. 37:15-19 1 Nephi 5:14 (Tribe of Joseph) 3 Nephi 10:17 (Tribe of Joseph) 2 Nephi 29:3-14 (A Bible!) John 10:16; 3 Nephi 15:21 (Other sheep...)	The more witnesses, the better. Instruction in Old Testament. In the mouths of 2 or more witnesses shall the truth be established. Example: Baptism 3 Nephi 11:23-26; Matt. 3:16; John 3:23; Acts 8:38 Eph. 4:5
3. Book of Mormon contradicts the Bible	3 Nephi 8:5, 12, 13, 19 3 Nephi 10:9 ("In the morning") Luke 23:44 (Crucifixion ends at 9th hr. – 3:00 p.m.	No contradiction – Book of Mormon and Bible agree on all important points. N.W. part of South America is 112° W. of Jerusalem - 112° is 7.5 hrs. – 3:00 p.m. minus 7.5 hrs. equals 7:30 "in the morning."
4. Book of Mormon fiction story by Joseph Smith – Spaulding manuscript	Articles of Faith By James E. Talmage Page 502	Not by any one man nor group of modern men. 180 new proper names. No contradiction. 3000 yrs. of history. Not even similar to Spaulding manuscript (see original at Oberlin College, Ohio).
5. Book of Mormon makes ridiculous statements	1 Nephi 13:30 Ether 1:42-43 Ether 2:8, 10, 12	Many statements, which seemed ridiculous in 1830 now proven true. Example: USA – "Nation above all nations," "Choice above all lands."
6. If Book of Mormon were true, would be more popular	Moroni 10:4 (Moroni's challenge)	More copies of Book of Mormon or Stick of Joseph sold than any other religious book except Bible. 55 English editions – 33 foreign editions. Very popular with anyone who will read with sincere desire to to know if true. Real power to conversion by itself. Example: Parley P. Pratt story.

CHARGES WILL NOT STAND UP.
RECORD IS TRUE, AUTHENTIC AND DIVINE!

ACT II
Internal Evidence

NOW LET'S GET into Act II of *The Trial of the Stick of Joseph.* This act, as you recall, covers defense by **Internal Evidence.** Remember Ezekiel tells us that two records are to work as one in the hands of the people and in the hand of God. (Ezekiel 37:15-19) Surely then, in the second great record, there should be some information or statement similar to this, and there is. There is a prophet on this (the American) continent speaking. He looked down the stream of time—he saw his own seed and the seed of his brother (the Lamanite people.)

> And it came to pass that I beheld the remnant of the seed of my brethren, and also the book of the Lamb of God, which had proceeded forth from the mouth of the Jew, that it came forth from the Gentiles unto the remnant of the seed of my brethren.
>
> *1 Nephi 13:38*

What book has come from the mouth of the Jew or the tribe of Judah, coming to the Gentile or the non-Jew, and then from them to the seed of this prophet's brethren (who would be the

Lamanites or the American Indians as we think of them today)? What book and what book only has come through those steps? The *Bible.* Then this *Book of Mormon* prophet is talking about the *Bible,* this "book of the Lamb of God."

> And they *(all men)* must come *(to him)* according to the words which shall be established by the mouth of the Lamb; and the words of the Lamb *(the angel tells this prophet)* shall be made known in the records of thy seed, as well as in the records of the twelve apostles of the Lamb; **wherefore they both shall be established in one;** for there is one God and one Shepherd over all the earth.
>
> *1 Nephi 13:41*

Do you see the same line of thinking? Two great records were to become as one in the hands of the people and God. The scripture goes on to say, "for there is one God and one Shepherd over all the earth." In other words, he is not just the God of the old continent, but the God of the new continent as well.

In line with this thought that the second record **did** make mention of the **oneness** of the two great records working as a team, let us read *Mormon, 7:8-9.* The prosecution claimed that this book was written under the influence of Satan. Everyone who has ever read the *Book of Mormon* and has attempted to show this has been in serious trouble. You cannot say that it is from Satan, because everywhere you turn it is evident the book comes from Jesus Christ.

> Therefore repent, and be baptized in the name of Jesus, and lay hold upon the gospel of Christ, which shall be set before you, not only in this record *(the Book of Mormon)* but also in the record which shall come unto the Gentiles from the Jews *(the Bible),* which record shall come from the Gentiles unto you.
>
> *Mormon 7:8*

Mormon is speaking to his own people yet unborn. The gospel is given not only in this record, the *Book of Mormon*, but also in the *Bible*. Now notice the oneness of the two great records.

> For behold, this *(the Book of Mormon)* is written for the intent that ye may believe that *(the Bible)*; and if ye believe that ye will believe this also; and if ye believe this ye will know concerning your fathers, and also the marvelous works which were wrought by the power of God among them.
>
> *Mormon 7:9*

Isn't that beautiful—two books working as a team?

The first charge in this second session: THE BIBLE IS THE WHOLE WORD OF GOD AND THEREFORE THE HEAVENS ARE CLOSED.

"Where in the world do you get that idea?" I asked.

"Well," they said, "turn to the very last chapter in the *Bible*, Revelation 22:18-19—the very last book and almost the very last verse."

> For I testify unto every man that heareth the words of the prophecy of this book, If any man shall add unto these things, *(Note this wording)* God shall add unto him the plagues that are written in this book:
>
> And if any man shall take away from the words of the book of this prophecy, God shall take away his part out of the book of life...
>
> *Revelation 22:18-19*

And so they said to me, "That does it. You can neither add to nor take away from the book of the word of God. The *Bible* then, is the whole word of God!"

It sounds logical, doesn't it? But when we looked at the facts, we found a number of discrepancies. First of all, when John wrote those words, was he writing in the *Bible?* No. There was not even a *Bible* in existence. What does "bible" mean? It comes from the word "biblia" which means, literally, "a library of small books." How many books are there in the King James Version? Sixty-six books—thirty-nine in the *Old Testament* and twenty-seven in the *New Testament.* All together, they make up sixty-six books. Now John was writing in just one of these sixty-six books, the book of *Revelation,* not in the "book of the *Bible."* So how could he have possibly meant by those words to seal and close a record which would be the combination of many small books many years later? Further, many of the greatest students of the *Bible* tell us that the book of *Revelation* should never have been placed last in chronology in the *New Testament,* but that other writings, including those of John himself, for instance, were later than the book of *Revelation.* Then I said, "If you are just bound and determined to use that line of interpretation on those two verses, let's go back to the *Old Testament, Deuteronomy 4:2.* Now we are way back in the beginning of the *Old Testament,* not even at the start of the *New Testament,* mind you, and almost the identical thought is given."

> Ye shall not add unto the word which I command you, neither shall ye diminish *ought* from it, that ye may keep the commandments of the LORD your God which I command you.
> *Deuteronomy 4:2*

I said to them, "It is almost the same wording, isn't it?" They were amazed. It is almost the same wording. "You can neither add to nor take from, according to this," I continued. "Since that is the case, let's rip out the rest of the *Bible."* There was a gasp that went through the mock court.

What if we did not have the rest of the *Old Testament* after *Deuteronomy?* What if we did not have the *New Testament* and its beautiful testimony of Christ's personal ministry? How much less we would know of the word of God!

We know, then, that John's words could not have been

interpreted as the prosecution had interpreted them. How should we then interpret them? The same identical way that we have been asked to interpret, in this day and age, modern-day revelation; for the commandment is still with us in modern times. When God has spoken to his prophets and caused them to write His words, it is not within the province of man to either take from those words or to add to those words; in other words, do not change the commandments of God with the words of man.

If we carefully compared over a thousand ancient copies of the *New Testament* in Greek, we would not find one solitary copy completely agreeing with any other one single copy. At that time there was no printed page like ours today. Copies were made the hard way, in long hand, and it was real easy to make errors, omissions or additions unless extreme caution was used.

What John the Revelator did mean was that when we copy, when we try to tell others of these things, we should try to stay with the original words and not put our own ideas in. How did these thousand copies of the *New Testament* become so different from one another? Sometimes the copier would be even as you and I. A woman from another church looked at my *Bible* once and said, "Mr. West, that is sacrilege." I had marginal notes; I had underlining; I had circling, I had personalized that *Bible* so that when I opened it to a certain page, something quickly told me that I had been there before. You do the same thing, I presume—personalize the books you study. We found the same thing in these Greek copies of the *New Testament*. But remember, those people did not have the printed page for a basis; they had to copy the scriptures the hard way. We find marginal notes by some of the copiers. When someone else copied from a copy that had been copied from a copy, they would not know whether a marginal note was something left out of the text and placed there in order that it would not be lost, or whether it was the private thinking or thought of the translator or copier. So sometimes we find marginal notes creeping into the text when they should not have been there. We find other thoughts that were completely omitted, maybe simply as unintentional errors of omission.

In any event, that is what John meant: When God had given a prophecy to a prophet, it was not within man's province to either add or detract from it as a prophecy. **Man** should not add. It did not say that God will not add, did it? To the book of which prophecy? Of "this" prophecy—not this prophecy of the total *Bible*, but this prophecy of the book of *Revelation*.

As further evidence, the terminology of the *Bible* itself shows us that neither is the *Bible* the whole word of God, nor are the heavens closed. Let us look at the record again. We find that God revealed everything from beginning to end, to prophet after prophet: to Adam, to Moses, Abraham and others. They would start to write these revelations and would get just so far, and God would stop them and say, in effect, "That is all you must write now. The people must learn to digest milk before they can learn to digest meat. The balance of this will be revealed to man, some-day, but the time is not yet. People must learn to walk before they can run." And then in the *Old Testament* we are told this—and it should be clear enough to individuals:

> Whom shall he teach knowledge? And whom shall he make to understand doctrine? *Them that are* weaned from the milk, and drawn from the breasts.
>
> For precept *must be* upon precept, precept upon precept; line upon line, line upon line; here a little, and there a little:
>
> *Isaiah 28:9-10*

Later Isaiah goes on to say that even with a foreign tongue will the Lord speak to his people.

> And thou shalt be brought down, *and* shalt speak out of the ground, and thy speech shall be low out of the dust, and thy voice shall be, as of one that hath a familiar spirit, out of the ground, and thy speech shall whisper out of the dust.
>
> *Isaiah 29:4*

Of course, God did not intend to close the heavens. The heavens have never been closed, except as man closes them within his own heart and says within himself. "I know I can't receive anything from heaven." Of course, that person cannot receive anything from heaven. Even in modern-day revelation Jesus Christ made it very clear that he was stopped from giving certain blessings to certain individuals because there was doubt in their hearts. Yes, you can close the heavens so far **as you** are concerned, if you wish, but God has not closed them, nor has he ever intended that the *Bible* be his whole word. Parts of the *Bible* itself are missing.

Then the prosecution said, "If there is anything missing from the *Bible,* it couldn't have been anything very important." Some of them were maintaining that even the punctuation marks were divinely placed. They had not reviewed recently the background of the King James Version of the *Bible,* had they? A great group of religious experts got together during the reign of King James in the hope that they could correlate their thinking as to what the proper translation should be. And they found that there was only one thing that they could really agree on and that was that they **disagreed;** and **when** they disagreed, they put the word or group of words in italics to show that there was disagreement among the experts as to how a certain word or phrase should be translated. I do not care what page you open to in the *Old* and *New Testaments,* almost without exception you will find italics there. In other words, there was disagreement as to how things were to be interpreted and what should be left in and what should be taken out.

Now let us see how important some of the things left out of the *Bible* were.

The background of the following scripture is that God had asked Moses to call the children of Israel together to read to them a certain book.

> And he took the **book of the covenant,** and read in the audience of the people: and they said, All that the Lord hath said will we do, and be obedient.
> *Exodus 24:7*

Surely there must have been many commandments. Surely it must have been vital to call all of the children of Israel together to have this book read to them. Now I can save you a little time. Do not search page by page carefully through the Bible looking for the "book of the covenant." It is not there! If the Bible is the whole word of God, where is this very important piece of scripture?

And is this all? If we wanted to, we could spend half an afternoon on this one point. Note, for example, the reference in Numbers 21:14, "the book of the wars of the Lord." Then go to 1 Chronicles 29:29. In practically one breath we are told of three books of scripture, and yet we find only one of them in the present-day Bible; two of them are missing.

> Now the acts of David the king, first and last, behold, they *are* written in the book of Samuel the seer, and in the book of Nathan the prophet, and in the book of Gad the seer,
>
> *1 Chronicles 29:29*

We read of two seers and one prophet. We have the book of Samuel the seer. We do not have the book of Nathan the prophet. It is missing. If it is scripture, and it is mentioned in the *Bible*, and it does not appear in the *Bible*, how could the *Bible* then be the whole word of God? Even in the *New Testament*, in *1 Corinthians 5:9*, in what we have assumed was the **very** first letter of Paul to the Corinthians, we find him making reference to a **previous** letter. Was it important? You bet it was important! Paul was calling the Corinthians to task; he was getting just a little bit irked at them because they had not followed up on the commandments that he had passed on to them from our Heavenly Father in the previous epistle. Now, if we have the first one, where is the number "0" epistle of Paul to the Corinthian saints?

No, the *Bible* is not complete. The heavens are not closed and never were intended to be, except as man would close them by closing his own heart. This would not seem strange to the world if they would look at the second great record. It testifies to us that certain things were to happen in this day and age—the latter-days—which would destroy part of the word of God.

> ...Thou hast beheld that the book proceeded forth from the mouth of a Jew *(the Bible)*; and when it proceeded forth from the mouth of a Jew it contained the plainness of the gospel of the Lord, of whom the twelve apostles bear record...
> And after they go forth by the hand of the twelve apostles of the Lamb, from the Jews unto the Gentiles, thou seest the foundation of a great and abominable church, which is most abominable above all other churches; for behold, *(now this is quite a charge)* **they have taken away from the gospel of the Lamb many parts which are plain and most precious;** and also many covenants of the Lord have they taken away.
> ...because of the many plain and precious things which have been taken out of the book, which were plain unto the understanding of the children of men, according to the plainness which is in the Lamb of God—because of these things which are taken away out of the gospel of the Lamb, **an exceeding great many do stumble,** yea, insomuch that Satan hath great power over them.
>
> 1 Nephi 13:24, 26, 29

Yes, of course, the things removed from the *Bible* were important. Why do we have over 700 Christian religions or factions of Christian religions? They all claim to believe the *Bible*. We find that exactly what the *Stick of Joseph* claimed would happen **did** happen, as a result of which "an exceeding great many do stumble."

Thus, we were able to answer the charge of the prosecution and prove to the satisfaction of the court that the *Bible* is **not** the whole word of God and that the heavens are **not** closed. Some further scripture would be important.

The second charge in the second session: ANOTHER BIBLE IS NOT NEEDED.

Upon presenting this thesis, the prosecution said, "You must admit that even tough the *Bible* doesn't seem to be the whole word of God, nor does it appear that the heavens were closed, you still must admit that another *Bible* is not needed."

Our answer to that charge was, "The more witnesses the better. Wasn't our case stronger because we had **twelve** men standing here before you as proxy witnesses, taking the place of the twelve personal witnesses, than if we had had **one only?** Turn to the *Bible* itself, *II Corinthians 13:1*. It tells us that, "In the mouth of two or three witnesses shall every word be established."

Two or more witnesses, always! Go into a court case with one witness and let another come in with two witnesses, and the chances are very good that you are going to get beaten, unless it can be shown that the two witnesses are not competent, honest, and so forth. In the mouths of two or more witnesses; two or more individuals; **two or more records;** two or more nations; if you please, two or more of the tribes of Israel. And I don't know what better we could do to answer this charge than to go to the words of Jesus Christ again. We find that he answered this charge even before it had been made. For he was showing one of his prophets on this continent, in ages past, that certain things would happen.

> And because my words shall hiss forth—many of the Gentiles shall say: A Bible! A Bible! We have got a Bible and there cannot be any more Bible.
>
> *2 Nephi 29:3*

LDS missionaries hear that statement time and time again out in the world. They hear it everywhere they turn. Now we go down in the sixth verse.

> Thou fool, that shall say: A Bible, we have got a Bible, and we need no more Bible. Have ye obtained a Bible save it were by the Jews?
>
> Know ye not that there are more nations than one? Know ye

not that I, the Lord your God, have created all men, and that I remember those who are upon the isles of the sea; and that I rule in the heavens above and in the earth beneath...

Wherefore murmur ye, because that ye shall receive more of my word? Know ye not that the testimony of two nations is a witness unto you that I am God, that I remember one nation like unto another? Wherefore, I speak the same words unto one nation like unto another. And when the two nations shall run together the testimony of the two nations shall run together also. *(Has it done so? It certainly has. The testimonies of the two nations do work together as one.)*

Wherefore, because that ye have a Bible ye need not suppose that it contains all my words; neither need ye suppose that I have not caused more to be written.

For I command all men...that they shall write the words which I speak unto them; for out of the books which shall be written I will judge the world, every man according to their works, according to that which is written. *(Now listen to His logic. Remember, Jesus Christ is speaking.)*

For behold, I shall speak unto the Jews and they shall write it *(the Bible);* and I shall also speak unto the Nephites and they shall write it; *(What tribe are the Nephites? The tribe of Joseph of Israel. Did they write? Yes, they wrote the Book of Mormon, or the Stick of Joseph as the Bible calls it.)* and I shall also speak unto the other tribes of the house of Israel, which I have led away, and they shall write it; and I shall also speak unto all nations of the earth and they shall write it.

2 Nephi 29:6-8, 10-12

How many other tribes? Ten. How many more Bibles to come? Some say it could be a combined thing, but as I read the whole text, I would assume that we could expect ten more writings—one for each of the other tribes. How many Bibles do you need before you are absolutely certain that Jesus **is** the Christ, Savior of the world, before you are certain that he has given us a beautiful blueprint for living that, if we will live by it, will bring peace and joy and harmony? How many do you need? Is one enough? Would two help you? Or are you going to be a little stubborn and wait until you get a half dozen before you really believe these things? Or are you going to be downright stubborn and wait until you have a dozen or more of them? Remember that Christ said that he would speak to all men—every nation—and they would write, and that when the nations would run together, the testimony would run together and grow together into an impregnable defense. *(See 2 Nephi 29:8.)*

Sometimes I become just a little bit alarmed. When I find, for instance, that the council of those who brought out the *Standard Revised Version of the Bible*—fully accepted by many of the Christian churches—included many men who were not even Christians, who wanted every reference to Jesus Christ as being the Son of God removed from the *Bible*, I became nervous. How far can we drift from the truth? They **did** succeed in removing all reference to Mary as being the **virgin** Mother of the Son of God. They got that far with their perfidy. How far can we drift from these things?

Now the Bible has told us that there were to be the two great books, one to be written for Judah, one written for Joseph. As we go through the *Book of Mormon* from *I Nephi 5:14,* on toward the end of the book, *3 Nephi 10:17,* and all in between, we find the constant repetition that these people are of the tribe of Joseph—the ones whose prophets are writing the religious record of this continent.

Do we then have another *Bible?* Well, I do not mind when people call the *Book of Mormon* the "Mormon Bible" if, in saying that, they do not thereby imply that because we have a *"Mormon Bible" we do not believe or use the other Bible.* Nothing, of course, could be farther from the truth. No people on earth, I feel, understand and appreciate the *Holy Bible* as do the members of The Church of Jesus Christ of Latter-day Saints. We understand it better **because** we have the second record. What were Mormon's words:

...that ye may believe that *(the Bible)*; and if ye believe that, ye will believe this *(Book of Mormon)* also...

Mormon 7:9

Then there were to be the two great records working as one.

I wish we could use an illustration here; maybe you can visualize one with me. Suppose we were to turn on one group of lights and then a second group of lights. Now let us assume that both groups of lights are identical in power. Think of the total illumination when both sets of lights are burning. Suddenly, we turn out the second group of lights. Is the first group of lights any less brilliant that it was before, in and of itself? No. It is still burning with the same brilliance, but because it has lost its running mate or teammate the total illumination has been drastically cut, hasn't it? Now, it is the same with the "Holy Bible Light" and the "Book of Mormon Light." If you turn off the "Book of Mormon Light" and put the "Holy Bible Light" on, or no matter how you work it, you get more total illumination when both great lights are working in unison than when either is working alone.

Think of two sets of brilliant lights working together—sixty-six books (the first set) in the "library of books" of the *Holy Bible*, and fifteen books (the second set) in the "library of books" of the *Book of Mormon*. The more illumination we have on any given problem today, the better. Some say, "We don't need another *Bible*." Choose any principle of the gospel you want; I wouldn't care what it was to be. Take the principle of love. It is a great law. Take the principle of faith or of fasting, or of the laying on of hands for the gift of the Holy Ghost, or take the Ten Commandments. It does not matter what principle you study. As you draw all you can from one of these two great records and then get all you can from the other, your total illumination is greatly enhanced when the two great records work as a team—as one in the hands of the people and as one in the hands of God, even as He intended. (See *Ezekiel 37:16-20; 2 Nephi 29:3-12.*)

I don't know what better example we could take than baptism, the very first outward ordinance of the gospel, one of the four cardinal principles of the gospel of Jesus Christ. I have often wondered how far afield we could drift from a beautiful, yet simple, principle. How far afield can we get? Let's recap a minute:

In the Christian churches of the earth there is baptism by immersion, baptism by sprinkling, baptism by dipping, baptism by the use of other liquids and not water, baptism with the use of no liquids. There is baptism by those who claim to have authority, baptism by those who claim no authority, baptism by those who claim that authority is not necessary. There is baptism with certain words being said, baptism with other words being said, baptism with no words being said. There is baptism that comes by just sitting and thinking upon it, and lo and behold, you're baptized! Now I wonder how far afield we can get on a simple subject.

Let us take the two great records and let them work as one in the hands of the people. Let us go, for instance, to the direct words of Jesus Christ, as recorded in the *Book of Mormon*, when he was here on this continent with these people. This scripture helps clarify the principle of baptism over which there seems to be so much confusion in the world.

> Verily I say unto you, that whoso repenteth of his sins through your words and desireth to be baptized in my name, on this wise shall ye baptize them—Behold, ye shall go down and stand in the water, *(Note that* **"stand in the water."** *Now that is going to be quite a trick, isn't it, if all you have is a cupful.)* and in my name shall ye baptize them.
>
> And now behold, these are the words ye shall say, calling them by name, saying:
>
> Having authority given me of Jesus Christ *(Apparently the authority **was** necessary then. Apparently this was to be done with certain things being said and done in His name.)* I baptize you in the name of the Father, and of the Son, and of the Holy Ghost. Amen.

And then shall ye **immerse** them in the water, and come forth again out of the water.

3 Nephi 11:23-26

I wonder how difficult we want to make it for ourselves, twisting such beautifully simple words. You remember that the Bible tells us that many people went to the River Jordan to be baptized "because there was much water there." (See *John 3:23*.) If all they needed was a cupful, why go to the River Jordan? They also went there because someone holding the authority to baptize was there. In this case, we are speaking of John the Baptist.

I was way up in the tops of the Andes Mountains on a recent trip. We zigzagged 38,500 miles, the equivalent of one and a half times around the globe, to get more Kodachrome pictures and covered every major Inca and pre-Inca ruin of the people of this continent that has been excavated to any extent, and then went on to Central America and North America. Way back there in the tops of the Andes, at the old ancient capital of the Incas, Cuzco, someone has built a fairly modern tourist hotel for people like me who go up there and want things a little easy between trips out into the wilderness country. On the wall of one of the rooms of the hotel is a beautiful mural. It depicts John the Baptist and Jesus Christ standing **ankle deep** in the water of the Jordan River while John pours a cupful of water over Jesus Christ. As I looked at the mural, I wondered how difficult we could make it for ourselves, twisting simple words and ideas. But now listen to the words of Jesus Christ again to the people on this continent, as recorded in the *Book of Mormon*. Apparently there had been some controversy upon this continent as to the method of baptism.

And according as I have commanded you thus shall ye baptize. And there shall be no disputations among you, as there have hitherto been; neither shall there be disputations among you concerning the points of my doctrine, as there have hitherto been.

3 Nephi 11:28

Oh, I wish we had a simple statement like that today in the *Bible*. I am sure it was there once upon a time, but remember, many of the plain and most precious things have been taken from the *Bible*. (See *I Nephi 13:26,29*.)

Do we need another *Bible*? Yes, we certainly do need another *Bible!* The more witnesses the better. The very commandments that Ezekiel received from God told us that we needed another great record—one stick for Judah, one for Joseph. Here we have the only answer on this point that has ever been given to the earth. No other people that I know of have even claimed to have the *Stick of Joseph* except The Church of Jesus Christ of Latter-day Saints. We know it is the *Stick of Joseph* because it is written about the Tribe of Joseph. We know it is the one spoken of to act "as one" with the other record, because if we read these various things, they **do** corroborate, substantiate and verify the *Bible*.

And so today in the *Book of Mormon* we have corroboration **plus**. I like to think of it that way—corroboration of the *Bible*, plus. Many things are made more clear. In the light of what we have learned about baptism from the *Book of Mormon*, let us turn back to the *Bible* record. We find that it does verify what the *Book of Mormon* has said. Turn to *Matthew 3:16; John 3:23; Acts 8:38; Ephesians 4:5.** Read them again in the light of what we have just read out of the second great record of the religious history of this earth. You will find that it does verify that the people went great distances to go where there was much water, that there were people holding authority to baptize, that even Jesus Christ, as pure as he was, knew that in order to fulfill all righteousness it was necessary to be baptized. You remember that John the Baptist questioned his own worthiness to baptize the Son of God, but Jesus insisted. And how was Jesus baptized? By immersion in water by one holding the authority.

---

* Note these and other scriptures recorded on the sheet of notes for the second lecture page 48.

Now we leave this second charge that another *Bible* was not needed with this thought: You remember one of the things that Jesus Christ said to his disciples on the old continent: "Other sheep I have, which are not of this fold..." *(John 10:16.)* and he told the people that he was to visit these other people and that there would be "one fold, and one shepherd." *(John 10:16.)* And when he came to this continent and appeared to these people in person he declared:

> And verily I say unto you, that ye are they of whom I said: Other sheep I have which are not of this fold; them also I must bring, and they shall hear my voice; and there shall be one fold, and one shepherd.
>
> 3 Nephi 15:21

This says, then, that these ancient people on the continent we now call America were the "other sheep" Jesus Christ was speaking of when he taught in the Bible lands. Of course, they did not understand what he meant when he said on the old continent that he had other sheep, and then on this continent, "...ye are they of whom I said: Other sheep I have..."

The third charge of the prosecution was: THE BOOK OF MORMON COULD NOT BE TRUE BECAUSE IT CONTRADICTS THE BIBLE.

Many times the prosecution attempted to show contradictions. We found there was no contradiction, but I admit on one point they had me in a corner. I had not been in the habit of flying all over the globe, I had not been in the habit of getting letters from my sons from all over the globe, I had not then been in seventy-seven different nations, so I was not as conscious as we are today of the various time elements in the earth. When they started reading to me out of the *Book of Mormon* beginning in *3 Nephi 8:5* and I kept asking them what in the world they were driving at, they said, "Now just sit still. You ought to be happy. We are reading from your book, and you shouldn't be nervous about it." And I didn't know what in the world they were driving at, but they started to read:

> And it came to pass in the thirty and fourth year, in the first month, on the fourth day of the month, there arose a great storm, such as one as never had been known in all the land.
>
> *3 Nephi 8:5*

Then they went on reading through the whole eighth chapter, through the ninth chapter—wading through the intricate stories into the tenth chapter and the ninth verse. Then they were ready to spring the trap. Well, this is what the scripture told.

Three hours of the most terrible destruction the people had ever known raged on this continent. The prophets of this continent testified to the people that during this identical period the Son of God was being crucified on the old continent, and our Heavenly Father was angry, and he was slaying many of the wicked of the earth. There was a terrible destruction on this continent. Whole cities of the wicked were seen to be destroyed in one stroke as the city ignited, apparently by spontaneous combustion, and every block of the city caught fire simultaneously. Other cities were caught up into the whirlwinds and never seen again. Still other cities dropped into a gash of the earth, and then the earth closed over them again. Eyewitnesses told these stories.

The prosecution waded through this, and I waited and I kept saying, "I can almost quote those words to you verbatim. Won't you tell me your point?"

"No, we won't—not yet."

And so they read of the three days and nights of darkness immediately following the three hours of destruction. And then they "sprang the trap."

...thus did the three days pass away. And it was **in the morning**...

3 Nephi 10:9

Then they went to Luke 23:44 in the *Bible,* and showed me that without any shadow of a doubt—and I couldn't refute it—Jesus Christ was crucified on the old continent between the sixth hour and the ninth hour, and that if you take this according to the timing of the Jews, starting as they did the first hour at sunrise, the sixth hour would be noon and the ninth hour would be **3 p.m.** they said, "There you are—a positive contradiction. The *Book of Mormon* says that the crucifixion ended in the morning and the *Bible* says it ended at 3 p.m.

I said, "Come again?" and then they went back with logic, very carefully, step by step, so that even I understood. Since the three days and nights **ended** in the morning, they must have started in the morning; since they immediately followed the three hours of destruction, the three hours of destruction **ended in the morning.** I had to admit that. And the prosecution said, "There is your contradiction." I had to admit that I had never noticed this apparent contradiction before.

I searched, and scrambled, and wrote, and telegraphed, to try and find the answer. Finally in the writings of Dr. James Talmage, himself a scientist, I found that he had noticed this discrepancy. He also noted that the writer in the *Book of Mormon,* as near as he could tell, was writing in the northwest part of present-day South America; and Luke was writing in Jerusalem; and that the northwest part of South America is 112° west of Jerusalem—or, in point of time, if it were 3 p.m. in Jerusalem, an identical timing would be 7:30 **"in the morning"** on this continent. Again, the prosecution wished they had never brought the matter up.

No, there is no controversy between the *Bible* and the *Book of Mormon.* On all points of important doctrine, they corroborate, substantiate, and vindicate each other.

The fourth charge of the prosecution was: THE *BOOK OF MORMON* CANNOT BE TRUE BECAUSE IT WAS SIMPLY A FICTION STORY BY JOSEPH SMITH.

How the prosecutors wished they had not made that statement! We brought experts in—philologists—who were not members of the Church. They had no ax to grind. They were expert scientists in the study of the use of words to express ideas. They testified at this mock trial, under oath—and they were actual experts—that if even an amateur who had never studied philology will read along in Nephi and get the manner of speaking, the method of expression of ideas, and then suddenly jump to the latter part of the *Book of Mormon* (the book of *Moroni*, or *Mormon* for instance) it will be self-evident that just one man did not write this book or develop the ideas coming from the book. Then these philologists went on to testify that the book gives evidence that many men had to do with the original work and the original ideas of the book.

Then the prosecution decided that Joseph Smith had some help; and they decided that one of the helpers was Oliver Cowdery. Oliver Cowdery testified in court that he did write the book with his own pen, remember? And again, they did not get the full statement; they just gave a part of the statement. It did sound on the surface, as though he were claiming to be the author of the book. But then when we got Oliver Cowdery's full statement into the trial, he said, "Sidney Rigdon didn't write the book. I wrote that book, almost in its entirety, with my own pen, **as the words fell from the lips of the Prophet,** as he received the impressions for the translation of the ancient records through the use of the ancient instrument, the Urim and Thummim." And again, the prosecuting attorneys wished they had no brought up the point.

Was it written by Sidney Rigdon? Did he have part in it? Time and time again, under oath, he testified that he had not even seen the *Book of Mormon* until it was handed to him in printed form after its publication. He had seen no part of the original at all. He was asked by his own son, almost on his deathbed, to testify once and for all on this point, and on his deathbed he again testified that he had never had any part in the formulation or translation or writing of the *Book of Mormon*.

No, it was not a fiction story.

Another supporting evidence of our defense was that we find over 300 proper names in the *Book of Mormon*, 180 had never been heard of before this book came off the press. Supposedly, they were brand new names. The scientists tell us, first of all, that it is impossible for one individual to make up 180 brand new names. They say that if you tried to do all the research work necessary, and so forth, you would go stark crazy. And I assure you, and you know, that Joseph Smith was not crazy. He was a marvelous prophet of God and leader of men in his day and age. Did a whole group of men make up these 180 supposedly new names? Now we know that they didn't because we have since run across tribe after tribe of Indians whose whereabouts were not known in1830 who have used those very names for centuries. And we say to some of these Indians way down in the jungle country, "How long have you called that river over there Nephihah?" And they say, "As long as we can remember—always Nephihah—from chief to chief, from father to son, passed down—always Nephihah." And we thought it was a new name. And we say to another tribe, "How long have you called that mountain over there Moronihah?" And they say to us, "Always Moronihah, from time of great quake when valley became high mountain." And we thought it was a new name in the year 1830. And so it was with most of these 180 supposedly new names, which came off the press in English print for the first time in 1830, with the publication of the *Book of Mormon*—they were names ages old, now generally known for the first time.

Now the prosecution, grabbing at straws, said, "Joseph Smith not only wrote a fiction story, but he stole the material," that old standby—the "stolen" Spaulding manuscript! I wonder how hard it is going to be to convince some people.

In 1884, President James H. Fairchild of Oberlin College, Ohio, and a Mr. Rice, a literary friend, were examining a heterogeneous collection of old papers and they found the lost Spaulding manuscript. After making a careful comparison of the manuscript and the *Book of Mormon*, they made public their results.

An article was published in the *New York Observer*, February 5, 1885, (fifty-five years after the publication of the *Book of Mormon*) in which President Fairchild said: "The theory of the origin of the *Book of Mormon* in the traditional manuscript of Solomon Spaulding will probably have to be relinquished... Mr. Rice, myself and others compared it (the Spaulding manuscript) with the *Book of Mormon* and could detect no resemblance between the two. Some other explanation of the *Book of Mormon* must be found, if any explanation is required." (*Articles of Faith*, James E. Talmage, p. 502.)

Remember, James H. Fairchild was the president of Oberlin College in Ohio, and was not a member of the Church. By making his statement he had nothing to gain, or any cause to support. How did he come across the original Spaulding manuscript? He testified that he found it in Honolulu, Hawaiian Islands, in the hands of a man who was originally a publisher in the area of Ohio where Spaulding lived. In two different court trials, enemies of Mormonism claimed, first, that Joseph Smith stole the Spaulding manuscript from the widow Spaulding, changed some of the names, and used it as a basis for the *Book of Mormon*. No evidence could be found against Joseph and so he was released. Then they claimed, second, that it was Sidney Rigdon who stole it. And Sidney Rigdon had not even seen the original manuscript of the *Book of Mormon* and had nothing to do with its translation or it's printing. It was proven that he could not possibly have been where the manuscript was supposed to have been at the time it was supposed to have been stolen, so he was released. Now as Dr.

Fairchild stated, the Spaulding manuscript was found. It has been printed twice at least, once by the Mormons in Salt Lake, and once by the Josephites of Ohio. I have a certified copy of it, and in case you have not read it, I assure you that it is not the original of the *Book of Mormon*. No, the *Book of Mormon* is **not** a fiction story by Joseph Smith, or any group of modern-day men. It is an actual religious history of this continent even as it claims to be.

The fifth charge of the prosecution was: IF THE BOOK WERE TRUE IT WOULD NOT MAKE SO MANY RIDICULOUS STATEMENTS.

Our answer: Many statements that sounded ridiculous in 1830 have since been proven completely true. We testify to the world that every statement still remaining in this book which has not yet come to pass is prophecy, and that it will come to pass just as surely as dozens upon dozens of prophecies have already come to pass since 1830.

We have to go along with the prosecution just a little bit though on this charge. Imagine a book coming off the press in 1830, and making a fantastic statement that in the latter-days the greatest nation upon the face of the earth would be built upon this continent. A youngster on the street today would not think that was a fantastic or ridiculous statement, would he? He would say, "Why anyone knows, even in the fifth grade, that that statement is true." But in 1830, they were still calling the United States "that great and foolish American **experiment.**" Europe didn't even give us the status of a nation. There was not a vestige of evidence in 1830 that there would be a nation on this continent greater than any nation upon the face of the earth in—"a land choice above all other lands." We find the evidence of this statement not only in *1 Nephi 13:30*, but also in the record of the people of Jared in *Ether, 1:42-43*, and *Ether 2:8, 10, 12.*

Let us go back about 124 years and get a quick picture. Chicago was known as little Ft. Dearborn, way out on the Western frontier, with sixty-five inhabitants, most of them military men who slept with their guns within their reach for fear the savage Indians would scalp them in their sleep. We had only three miles of steam railway. We were so poor as a nation that the president and his cabinet had to borrow on their personal finances to pay the cost of government in the year of 1830. In that year, many of our people went hungry because we did not raise enough food to feed them in this land that was supposed to be a choice land above all other lands.

Now let us get the comparison today in this land of the United States, with only 1/20th of the landed area of the world and only 1/16th of the population of the world. Even after World War I, we were producing 1/3 of all of the coal, doing 1/3 of all the manufacturing of the earth, producing 1/2 of all the steel of the earth, 2/3 of the cotton, and 4/5 of the corn. We had 1/4 of all the wealth of the earth, did 1/3 of all the banking, had 1/2 of all the railroads of the earth, and did 1/2 of all the printing in the earth. Chicago was not way out on the "Western frontier" but in the eastern part of our nation. Its sixty-five inhabitants had grown to over three million. We had over 350,000 miles of steam railways instead of three. The closest nation to us was over 200 billion dollars behind us in national wealth. We have recently just finished "hitching our belts" to feed a good part of the world with our surplus. Yet it was sixty-eight long years after this prophecy was made in the *Book of Mormon* before we even stepped into fourth place among the nations of the earth—after the war with Spain; then in 1904, into second place after the Russo-Japanese agreement; and it was nearly one hundred years after the prophecy was made, after World War I ended in 1917, before we stepped into first place as a nation of the earth. The statement in the *Book of Mormon* that "the greatest nation" of the earth would be built on this land choice above all other lands sounded fantastic in 1830. Today we know it is absolutely true.

Now in our next session, we will spend the entire session showing "ridiculous statements" made by the *Book of Mormon*, in the year 1830, coming true with visual proof and with the evidence of the scientific men of the earth right before us. The external evidence is coming forth so fast that we cannot keep up with it.

The prosecution brought up this point; we didn't. **They** were the ones who said that the book makes ridiculous statements and in answer to that charge we gave endless evidence to the contrary, until they wondered how they were ever going to get our answers to that charge shut off.

The sixth charge of the prosecution was: IF THE *BOOK OF MORMON* WERE TRUE IT WOULD BE MORE POPULAR.

This was an accusation of a desperate prosecution. Remember they were going down for the third time; they had tried everything they could think of to prove fraud in the bringing forth of the *Book of Mormon*, and there was no proof. The book was and is true, authentic, and divine! Now they said that if the book were true, it would be more popular.

Our answer to that charge is twofold. First, what does truth necessarily have to do with popularity? Many times because a thing is true it is unpopular. Isn't that true? Then the second part of our answer was posed as another question, "How popular can a book get?" We used the terminology of the charge. There has never been a religious book come off the press, which has outsold the *Book of Mormon* (stick of Joseph) except its running mate, the *Holy Bible* (stick of Judah). That's a fact! The *Book of Mormon* has topped all other religious books except the Bible by an immense margin. Until many of the churches accepted the *Standard Revised Version of the Bible*, which gave great impetus to sales of the *Bible*, the *Bible* was neither gaining greatly nor losing greatly in sales; it was somewhat static, while the *Book of Mormon* was gaining by leaps and bounds. The *Book of Mormon* is extremely popular with anyone who will read it with a real desire to know whether or not it is true.

As an evidence of the popularity of this great *Book of Mormon* in the world today and in times past, I would like to give an example of just one copy of the *Book of Mormon*, and how popular it became with a certain group of people.

You remember we introduced Samuel H. Smith as the first missionary for the Church. He had a rough time. He went from door to door, but ministers had advised their people ahead of time not to talk to Mormon missionaries, because the book that they had was founded under the influence of Satan. So he thought that if he could get to one of the popular ministers of the day perhaps the minister would help him get into the homes of his people. He was sure that if he could get a minister to read the *Book of Mormon*, he would realize that it was not written under the influence of Satan. Samuel Smith tells of going to the home of Reverend John P. Green, a very well known Methodist minister. Reverend Green was away from home, but Samuel talked to his wife. She said, "Oh, I wouldn't dare have the *Book of Mormon* in the house. I have heard of Joe Smith and his 'Gold Bible', and my husband says it was written under the influence of Satan."

Well, he gave up trying to sell the book to her. In fact he was out of the gate about to leave, and then he said that he was deeply impressed to go back and **give** her a copy of the book. He went back and said, "Mrs. Green, I know you are a very intelligent person, and I know you do not mean to be unfair in any regard. Do you think it is quite fair to condemn a thing before you have even looked at it?"

It made her stop and think a minute and she said, "No, I guess that isn't very fair."

Then he turned to *Moroni 10:4*, to the beautiful words of Moroni, a veritable challenge to anyone who would receive the book to test its truth.

And when ye shall receive these things, I would exhort you that ye would ask God, the Eternal Father, in the name of Christ, if these things are not true; and if ye shall ask with a sincere heart, with real intent, having faith in Christ, he will manifest the truth of it unto you, by the power of the Holy Ghost.

Moroni 10:4

Samuel said that Mrs. Green choked up and through her tears said, "That certainly doesn't sound as if it were written under the influence of Satan, does it?" She said, "I want to admit that I have wanted to read that book and if you care to leave it, I promise that I will."

Samuel went back to this home a short time later, and again the Reverend was out among his people. Samuel did not get to talk to him in person, but he said to Mrs. Green, "Did you read the book?"

And she said, "Yes, and I believe every word of it." Samuel was elated and he said, "Well, what does the Reverend think about it?"

She said, "Oh, I didn't even dare tell him that I had it in the home because I knew it would just cause trouble."

"Please Mrs. Green, I am pleading with you to get your husband to read that book, because I believe he can help us eliminate some of the prejudice in this area." She finally agreed that she would do her best—and you fellows know how these "girls" of ours have a way of getting at us—like water dripping upon a stone and pretty soon there is a hole in the stone!

"One day in desperation," Reverend Green testified later, "I grabbed that book out of my wife's hand and said, 'Give me that thing and I will show you in the very first two pages I open to, that it was written under the influence of Satan.'" But he was in trouble! He could not show that. He read the two pages that he happened to turn to, and then he said, "I turned to the first of the book and I read the testimony of those witnesses, and then I went through the entire book, page by page, reading word by word. When it came time to eat, I didn't want to eat, when it came time to sleep, I didn't want to sleep, I didn't want to talk to anybody. All I wanted to do was read." And he testifies that he read the book from cover to cover before he ever laid it down.

Now he was completely converted by the power of conversion of the *Book of Mormon* itself. He resigned his position as Reverend in the Methodist Church and brought a good many of his flock into the restored Church after he was baptized into The Church of Jesus Christ of Latter-day Saints.

Now continuing the story of this one copy of the *Book of Mormon*, Reverend Green handed the self-same book that had converted his wife and himself to Phineas Young, who was on one of the councils of the Methodist Church, and he said to Phineas, "I don't want to tell you anything about the book. Just read it and let me know what you think about it." And the same thing happened to Phineas. He was converted, and he resigned from the Methodist group and joined the restored Church. Phineas handed it to his brother Brigham Young, and he said, "Brigham, I want you to read this book and let me know what you think about it." Brigham read the book, and he was converted and later became one of the great presidents of the Church, following the Prophet Joseph Smith. Brigham gave it to his sister, Mrs. Murray, and she was converted. Her daughter later married Heber C. Kimball, as I recall. And then Brigham went to his sister and said, "Have you finished that book?" And she said, "Yes, I have." "Well let me have it. I have some work to do with it." He did not know his way around the Church as well as he later did, and he went on a mission way up into Canada before he was even baptized into the restored Church. There he met his brother John, who was on a mission for the Methodist church, and he said to John, "John, here is a book. I want you to read it, and let me know what you think about it." So John read the book, and he resigned his work as a missionary for the Methodist group and joined the Church. (See *History of the Prophet Joseph Smith*, by Lucy Mack Smith, pp. 167-168.)

Now that is the story of one copy of the *Book of Mormon* and how popular it became with the people of the earth. There have been fifty-five English editions, thirty-three foreign editions, and it has been translated into many, many tongues. It is **extremely** popular with anyone who will read it with real intent to know whether or not it is the word of God.

The charges will not stand up! The *Book of Mormon* is true, authentic and divine! May you have a strong and burning testimony of the truthfulness of this work, I humbly pray in the name of Jesus Christ. Amen.

Prologue to
ACT III

MAY I REMIND YOU that we are reviewing a case in which the Stick of Joseph (*Book of Mormon*) was on mock trial under conditions approximating a courtroom to every possible degree. Our old professor of law had been a judge for many years, and our test for the year was to try a case within all limits of legal procedure. So each student in the class had the "privilege", as the judge called it, (we called it many other names later) of defending or prosecuting some law case **against the entire balance of the class.**

While studying law, I was also studying and teaching the *Book of Mormon*. As I did so, and as my legal knowledge increased, I became more and more convinced that God himself had indeed briefed a case for the authenticity of the "Stick of Joseph" as the *Bible* called it (See *Ezekiel 37: 15-19*) or the *Book of Mormon* as the world knows it. So I thought to myself, "If you are going to be tested, what better could you do than get the Lord on your side?" So I took the case for the authenticity of the *Book of Mormon*. You see, I had a firm and burning testimony in my heart that the *Book of Mormon* was true, and I felt sure the evidence would bear me out.

When I selected this case and decided to defend the Stick of Joseph (*Book of Mormon*) against the charge of fraud, the opposition was elated. These young, "budding attorneys" were certain, when they learned that the Stick of Joseph was in reality the *Book of Mormon*, they could win the case in a very short time, prove it completely fictitious and the work of the imagination of some poor farmer school boy who had not even approached the eighth grade. Perhaps they were overly enthusiastic and too sure of themselves. I must admit however, they brought things into the courtroom that I did not have the least idea existed—things that appeared to be evidence against the authenticity of the book. I had not realized, as many to whom I have spoken in the Church have not realized, that over 1,500 books had been written as commentaries on the *Book of Mormon* and many of those 1,500 books had been written specifically **against** the *Book of Mormon*. So time and time again the prosecution brought in evidence which **seemed** conclusive in bringing out a fraudulent nature of the *Book of Mormon*. But, as we got to the facts and sifted away the hearsay, the conjecture, the guesswork— as we forgot about those things and those people who **thought** that someone had said, or thought that someone had heard that someone had thought that someone had said (and it got that ridiculous in some cases), when we got down to prime witnesses, competent witnesses, people who personally had to do with the thing we were talking about, we found there **was no** evidence against the *Book of Mormon*. Time and time again something which seemed to be against it, like the old boomerang from the land "way down under" swung around and hit the prosecution in the back of the neck, as it returned home to the senders with evidence that damaged rather than strengthened their case.

Most of these mock trials had lasted a day or two, a week at the very most, but this one went on for two weeks and was into the third week of trial. After the concluding arguments, the judge rendered his decision in favor of the defense and said to the prosecution, "You have not even established a toe hold, much less a foothold, in breaking down the marvelous evidence for the authenticity of the Stick of Joseph."

Then the judge called me into his office and said, "Jack, where in the world did you get the evidence you presented in this mock trial?"

I grinned at him and said, "Well, I told you in court that I did not take credit for one particle of this evidence. It isn't new. It has been available for the most part, many years, to anyone who wanted to look it up. I believe with all my heart that God himself has set up this evidence, and I told all of you that in the courtroom."

The judge said, "I want to tell you that in all my years in the law I don't think I have heard a law case more nearly perfect than this one. But I wouldn't have given you a plugged nickel for your chances of proving that book to be true through legal procedure.

Now, we have had two of the three lectures on *The Trial of the Stick of Joseph*. First, we examined the **personal witnesses** and the testimonies of twelve men, all of whom declared that they saw and handled the ancient golden records from which the Prophet Joseph Smith translated the *Book of Mormon*. In some cases, they saw these things and heard them under supernatural conditions. We investigated their lives and found that not one of them ever betrayed his testimony or turned against it, and yet we found almost ideal conditions existing for a betrayal, if this thing had been a fraud.

In the second lecture we let the *Book of Mormon* answer for itself, with **internal evidence,** a whole group of charges made by the prosecution against the book and against those who brought it forth. We found that it was its own best witness—that it could answer the charges of the world against it. We found that there was a "oneness" between the *Book of Mormon* (Stick of Joseph) and the *Bible* (Stick of Judah) as we compared them back and forth with each other, even as had been promised in the *Old Testament*.

Let's turn again to *Ezekiel 37:15-19*. We go to this every once in a while. I love this, and I think it sets the stage for the necessity of, indeed, the very commandment of God that there should be such a record as the Stick of Joseph.

The word of the LORD came again unto me, saying,

Moreover, thou son of man, take thee one stick, and write upon it, For Judah, and for the children of Israel his companions: then take another stick, and write upon it, For Joseph, The stick of Ephraim, and for all the house of Israel his companions:

And join them one to another into one stick; and they shall become one in thine hand. *(Evidently the Lord wanted to be sure that nobody misunderstood, so he repeated somewhat, in the next verse.)*

And when the children of thy people shall speak unto thee saying, Wilt thou not shew us what thou meanest by these?

Say unto them, Thus saith the LORD GOD; Behold, I will take the **Stick of Joseph,** *(Joseph of Israel)* which is in the hand of Ephraim, and the tribes of Israel his fellows, and will put them with him, even with the Stick of Judah, and make them one stick, and they shall be one in mine hand.

Ezekiel 37:15-19

Remember, when I asked the prosecution where the Stick of Judah was, there was no hesitation. I am sure any student of the Bible would agree that the *Holy Bible* is the Stick of Judah. That it is the religious and the scriptural record of the tribe of Judah.

Now, some have thought that the *New Testament* was the Stick of Joseph, but that could not be, for its main character was Jesus Christ, the Son of God. From which tribe of Israel did Christ descend? He descended from Judah of Israel, not Joseph, and so the idea that the *New Testament* was the Stick of Joseph would not hold.

I asked the prosecution, "Do you have the Stick of Joseph, the religious record of the tribe of Joseph?" Well, you remember, they didn't happen to have the Stick of Joseph right there handy, but they were sure that they could get it. So they went to their ministers, and their rabbis, and their priests, and they came back empty-handed. They said, "That's peculiar, our people don't know anything about the "Stick of Joseph."

"Well," I said, "then you wouldn't object very much, would you, if I placed the Stick of Joseph in this case as exhibit 'A'?"

They looked at it and said, "But that book says the *Book of Mormon*. How can it be the Stick of Joseph?"

And I said, "Well, this says the Holy Bible. How can it be the Stick of Judah?" And they got the point. We know it is the Stick of Judah because when we read the text we find it is God's dealings particularly with the tribe of Judah. By the same test, as you read this *Book of Mormon*, you will find, although it is called today the *Book of Mormon*, that it is literally the religious record of the tribe of Joseph, thus the Stick of Joseph.

Now, in this session (the third lecture) we are going to spend three hours with the experts, including the showing of 117 Kodachrome slides, selected from over 4,000 slides of the ancient ruins of this continent, which I have personally taken. We are going to the finest leaders in the fields of archaeology, zoology, ethnology, philology and anthropology to get their testimony regarding their findings in the Americas. We are going to stay completely with scientists who are not members of the Church. I have consistently felt that our case was stronger if we stayed with those experts who have no interest in proving the *Book of Mormon* true, indeed, who in many cases, I am sure, have no intention of proving any part of the *Book of Mormon* true by giving their testimonies. But if, as we go to their expert knowledge and testimony we find that they are **verifying** the story of the *Book of Mormon*, if as we explore the ruins on this continent of two of the greatest nations ever to occupy the earth (up to their individual times)—if we find these things **substantiating** the *Book of Mormon*, surely that should be wonderful external evidence for the authenticity of the book.

For quick and easy reference at this time, we are going to use just one reference volume for our quotations, *The Americas Before Columbus*, by Dewey Farnsworth.

Now, at the outset, may I caution you on two points.

First: Although the *Book of Mormon* tells of two **main** groups of people who migrated to this country in very early times, nowhere does it say that there were not others; in fact, it mentions a third group, the Mulekites, and undoubtedly there have been still other migrations.

Second: Not all scientists are agreed as to what these ancient ruins on this continent mean, and what the things they find here imply, but as we go to some of the greatest men in their fields, we find them coming closer and closer, year by year, to an agreement that falls right into line with the testimony of the *Book of Mormon*.

I have been what some may call an "armchair archaeologist" for about twenty-five years (I can give a lot of "advice" from the sidelines, but I'm too lazy to do the digging,) and I have been thrilled by the things the experts have said about the archaeology, ethnology, etc., of this continent. I do not set myself up as a scientific expert and if I am an expert at all, it's an "expert on the experts." I have very carefully followed the testimony of the scientists for over twenty-five years. I have watched, as many have, how time after time scientists have swung around, point by point, until they are right in line with what the *Book of Mormon* says. I have a testimony of the truth of the *Book of Mormon*, as I am sure most of you have, and I do not feel at all chagrined to refer to those experts who are agreeing with the *Book of Mormon* and use their quotes very freely. If there are a few who still do not completely agree with the *Book of Mormon*, then I just by-pass them, knowing that as they learn more about these ancient civilizations their opinions will change step by step, until soon they are right in line with the *Book of Mormon* line of thinking, and that has happened countless times.

ACT III
EXTERNAL EVIDENCE

CLAIMS OF THE BOOK OF MORMON	REFERENCES	EXTERNAL EVIDENCES	
1. Peopled by two main groups Jaredites – 2200 B.C. Nephite-Lamanites 600 B.C.	Title Page of the *Book of Mormon*	Lowry (4) Galatin (10) Bancroft (10) Brinton (6) Jordan (6)	Spinden (12) Putnam (17) Combined Statement (3)
2. Had Laban's plates of brass	*1 Nephi 3:3-4*	DeRoo (41) Colton (26) Lee (21)	DeRoo (65) Kingsborough (18)
3. Christ appeared on this continent after his resurrection	*3 Nephi 11:8-10*	Rosales (36) Kingsborough (36)	DeRoo (41) Brinton (42)
4. Wrote on Gold Plates in Reformed Egyptian and Hebrew	*Mosiah 8:9* *Mormon 9:32*	Saville (65) Picture (60) Willard (140)	Jones (22) Jones (18) Marett (22)
5. Built with cement	*Helaman 3:7-9*	Picture (55) Willard (38)	Gann (39)
6. Hardened copper	*Jarom verse 8*	Bradford (140) Charnay (142)	Nadaillac (142) Picture (150)
7. Had machinery and wheels	*Jarom verse 8* *3 Nephi 3:22*	Picture (39) Picture (94) Picture (38)	Poindexter (116) Mason (124)
8. Had horses and elephants	*Enos verse 21* *Ether 9:17-19*	Brea Tar Pits L.A. County Museum (Skeletons)	Times Ency. (157) Ency. Brit. (158) New Amer. Ency. (156) Murray (157)
9. Great cities Dense population Large buildings	*Alma 50: 13-15* *Ether 10:20-21*	Morley (104) Mason (78) Picture, Palenque (58)	Picture, Chichen Itza (6)
10. Sunken and destroyed cities	*3 Nephi 8:5 – 9:2*	Bancroft (41) Baldwin (41) Spinden (57)	Gann (72) Picture (63)

NOTE: For ease of reference, numbers in parentheses refer to pages in The Americas Before Columbus by Farnsworth where quotes of these experts also appear.

BIBLIOGRAPHY
(In order of the quotations above.)

Farnsworth, The Americas Before Columbus (see note above)
Lowry, Schoolcraft's Enthnological Researches, Vol. 3
Galatin, Bancroft's Native Races, Vol. 5, p. 19
Bancroft, Native Races, Vol. 5, pp.20-22, 210
Brinton, American Hero, pp. 145-146 and
   Religions of Primitive Peoples, p. 251
Jordan, Americans, p. 21
Spinden, Ancient Civilizations of Mexico, pp. 75, 49
Putnam, Prehistoric Remains of the Ohio Valley, and
   Century Magazine article, March 1890
DeRoo, History of America Before Columbus, pp. 41, 65
Colton, Origin of the American Indians,
Kingsborough, Mexican Antiquities, Vol. 6, p. 401
   and Vol. 8, p.3, Scrpas, p. 277
Lee, The Great Migration, p. 63
Rosales, History of Chile
Saville, The Goldsmith's Art in Ancient Mexico, p. 175
Willard, City of the Sacred Well, pp. 134, 88-90

Marett, Archaeological Relics in Mexico, p. 29
Thompson & Gann, People of the Serpent,p. 228
Bradford, American Antiquities, pp. 158-159
Jones, History of Ancient America, p. 126
Charnay, Ancient Cities of the New World, p. 69
Nadaillac, Pre-Historic America, p. 181
Grāna Reyes, Time Magazine article, Oct. 26, 1953, p. 54
   (Regarding hardened copper)
Pointdexter, The Ayar-Incas, pp. 230-231
Mason, Columbus Came Late, pp. 198, 64
Murray, Man's Unknown Ancestors, pp. 47-49
Encyclopedias, Brittanica (ancient horses, elephants) Times
Ency. & Gazetteer, Vol. 4
New Americanized Ency., Vol. 5, p. 3197
Morley, Carnegie Institue Bulletin, No. 57 (1915)
   and No. 219 (1920)
Baldwin, Ancient America, p. 176
Gann, Maya Cities, Ancient Cities, pp. 99-100

ACT II
External Evidence

NOW WITHOUT FURTHER review and summation let us call in the experts to testify in what we term Act III of The Trial of the Stick of Joseph—(defense by EXTERNAL EVIDENCE.)

The prosecution had charged that the *Book of Mormon* could not be true because it made so many ridiculous statements. How they wished they had not made that charge! Our answer was that many statements, which sounded ridiculous in the year 1830, had since been proven true. And I testify to you that any statements in the *Book of Mormon* which even now sound fantastic, are prophecies and they will yet be proven true. We have given in Act II just one example of a "ridiculous" statement, which has come true. Now we will continue.

Let us go to a whole group of claims of the *Book of Mormon*, which, when the book first came off the press (1830), sounded fantastic beyond belief. You will have to go back with me over a hundred years before some of these things sound fantastic.

The **FIRST CLAIM** that we will consider today is the story of the book, that this continent in early times was **PEOPLED BY**

TWO MAIN GROUPS. Remember, the *Book of Mormon* does not claim that the two main groups of people were the only ones ever to come to this continent. The book tells us that the first great group of people were the Jaredites, coming from the Tower of Babel at the time of the confusion of tongues. That was about 2200 B.C. The book is not quite clear as to which ocean this first group crossed in coming to America. All we know from the record is that the Jaredites went northward out of the valley of Shinar in Asia, then into an area where man had not "hitherto been" to a minor sea on which they traveled for some time before reaching the shores of the great sea. I have felt, and I give it to you as my personal thinking only, that they went westward to the Mediterranean Sea and then to the Atlantic, for had they gone Eastward they would surely have been in an area where men had theretofore been. Therefore, they would have come across the Atlantic Ocean, and this, I believe, checks with the Indian legends. We do know that they landed somewhere north of "the narrow neck of land" as they have called it in the *Book of Mormon*, the narrow neck between the continent to the north and the continent to the south. The narrow neck, then, was the dividing point, and somewhere north of that point they landed.

The Jaredites became a tremendous nation, according to their record as it is given in the *Book of Mormon*. Jesus Christ testified that it would be the greatest nation up to that time on the face of the earth. They peopled the northern part of the land sea-to-sea and coast-to-coast, keeping the southern part mainly for a hunting ground. They had been promised if they kept the word of God, they would prosper in the land; if they did not, they would be destroyed and another people would take their place.

We find that these Jaredites lived on the American continent a long period of time. The closing year of their history is a little vague, but there seems to be, as near as we can tell, an overlap with the history of the second great group of people. Some men from Zarahemla (people of the second group) accidentally found

Coriantumr, a surviving Jaredite. Coriantumr lived with the people of Zarahemla "for the space of nine moons," or nine months as the Indian's moon terminology would be. (See *Omni verse 21.*) Thus we see that there must have been an overlap in the histories of these two groups of people.

Now, let's assume a figure of approximately 500 B.C. as the closing of Jaredite history. That figure may be adjustable one way or the other. They had, in other words, approximately 1,700 or 1,800 years of history on this continent. They were a marvelous people, a great nation. The Jaredites were the greatest nation of any nation up to their time on the face of the earth. That would put the Jaredites ahead of the civilization of ancient Egypt and China.

The second group of people came from Jerusalem in the year 600 B.C. They crossed the ocean we now call the Pacific, landing as nearly as we can tell from the records, somewhere on the west coast of Chile or thereabouts on the South American continent. This second group of people known as the Nephite-Lamanite nation also became the greatest nation up to **their** time on the face of the earth, according again to the testimony of Jesus Christ given in the *Book of Mormon*. That would put them ahead of the civilizations of Rome and Greece, in contemporary nations.

Do you know how fantastic these statements sounded in the year 1830? Do you remember the charge of the prosecution that the book could not be true because it made so many ridiculous statements? Since the prosecution had brought up the point, we could take all the time we wanted in defense, so we gave them evidence upon evidence upon evidence in answer to this charge. The book if filled with countless statements, which sounded fantastic in the year 1830, but today they have been proven to be completely true.

There were no scientists in the year 1830 who claimed that two main groups of people came by migration to this land in early times. There were no scientists who claimed that the great migrations in both cases came by sea voyage. There were no scientists who claimed that the great majority of the inhabitants of this continent in early times had been other than native to this land. The scientists thought that the people who had migrated had come across the top of the continent over the Siberian area (by which name we know it now), the Aleutians, Alaska, Canada and down through that territory. Some are still claiming migrations came in this way and undoubtedly some did, but not the two great ones.

We will follow the presentation organized by Dewey Farnsworth in *The Americas Before Columbus,* a book in which have been compiled many interesting facts from authoritative sources. At the end of each quotation from a scientist will be given the reference to the original source material. The bibliography in this publication will give the reference source also if you have a copy of the book, follow along as the pages are mentioned.

First of all we will turn to page 4 of *The Americas Before Columbus* which quotes an ethnological report by Lowry wherein he offers a "reply to official inquires respecting the aborigines of America." He concludes "That the first settlement was made shortly after the confusion of the building of the Tower of Babel." That is the same time the *Book of Mormon* stated that the Jaredites landed in America.

On page 10 we read, "Professor Waterman of Boston says of the progenitors of the American Indian: 'When and whence did they come? Albert Galatin, one of the profoundest philologists of the age, concluded that, so far as language afforded any clue, the time of their arrival could not have been long after the dispersion of the human family.'" Again we read a scientific reference to early American settlers near the time of the Tower of Babel, at which time the "dispersion of the human family" occurred.

On this same page there is a quote from Herbert Howe Bancroft, the greatest historian of our time, particularly regarding the history of these nations and people on this continent, "Toltecs claim to have come to America at the time of confusion of tongues...The Yucatans have a tradition that they came originally from the far east, passing **through** the sea." One of the seemingly fantastic statements in the

Book of Mormon was that the first great group of people, the Jaredites, came to this continent in ships, which are described somewhat as we would today describe submarines. I think I can almost hear the words an expert shipbuilder would have said in the year 1830, as he read the *Book of Mormon*: "Well now, there are lots of things that I can believe, lots of things that make wonderful sense to me in this book, but when you come to this story about ships, you are talking about my specialized field, and everyone knows that a ship can't be built that will travel under water." Well now, we know that everyone knows a ship can be built that will travel under water, don't we? And since Jared and the brother of Jared stated many times that God was directing the construction of these ships, surely He knew enough then to show them how to build ships which a common ordinary man can built today.

All right, so the Indian legend now as to the first people was that they came from the Far East. That would mean then that they would come across what we now know as the Atlantic Ocean, coming **through** the sea.

"The Olmec traditions," Bancroft goes on to say, "relate that they came by sea from the East. The Algonquins preserve a tradition of a foreign origin and sea voyage. They offered an annual thank offering for a long time in honor of their safe arrival in America."

Let us now go to page 6 of *The Americas Before Columbus.* D.G. Brinton tells us here, "The Mayas... claimed that their ancestors came from distant regions in **two** bands. The largest and most ancient immigration was from the East across, or rather, **through the ocean.** The **second** band less in number and later in time came from the West..." Is that tying in with the *Book of Mormon*? It certainly is!

Also on page 6, Emil Leopold Jordan tells us, "The best authorities agree that no human race is indigenous to the new world." Then he explains what he means. "Every human being that has ever lived in America has been an immigrant or the descendant of an immigrant."

Now let us discuss the **second** great group of people. And for this purpose, let's read a statement by Dr. Spinden of Peabody Institute, perhaps the greatest authority on the chronology of the ancient people of this continent. He, together with Dr. Morley of Carnegie Institute, claimed to have found a stone, about a third of which they were able to decipher as to the hieroglyphic writing. They believe that it tells the story of the first landing of the second great group of people, and through the chronology of Dr. Spinden, he thinks he has been able to establish the date they arrived. His testimony is on page 12.

> With records cut in imperishable stone, the Mayas suddenly made their appearance upon the historical scene on August 6, 613 B.C. Why on August 6, 613 B.C.? Where were the Mayas on August 5th? Nobody knows... They might as well have dropped down from Mars or some other planet on the 6th day of August.
> Quoted from *Popular Science*

Someone should tell Dr. Spinden that somebody **does** know— somebody **does** know **where** they were, **who** they were, **where they came from,** why they came, what happened to them after they came and what **finally** happened to them—because somebody has the religious history of these people on this continent and the source of their origin. But well might Dr. Spinden say that "they might as well have dropped down from Mars or some other planet." They **did** drop down from somewhere—they dropped down out of the waves of the sea. And the waves of the sea leave no tracks, do they? In other words researchers find no **land** migration marks or tracks of this people.

With this discussion, we can accept the possibility then that there were **two major groups.** Professor F.W. Putnam, in an article entitled "Prehistoric Remains in the Ohio Valley," published in *Century Magazine*, March 1890, said: "It has been stated by eminent students of American archaeology that two distinct classes of mankind inhabited this continent in early times. I would like to be even more definite in this assertion that one of these ancient races spread from the north portion of the continent (the Jaradites), and the other from the south portion." This second group was no doubt the Nephite group, which was eventually divided into the Nephites (the white skinned brothers) and the Lamanites (the dark skinned brothers). In the conflicts between these two groups, the darker people constantly pushed the white people farther and farther north until they came to the land they called Desolation.

They did not want to go in to that land because there were great mounds of human bones. Another people had fought a war so fierce and so rapidly that apparently they did not even have time to bury their dead. And the land was burned off. There were no trees in the area to speak of, so when the Nephites were finally pushed into this area by their dark skinned apostate brothers, they had to turn to building material other than wood, and that brings up another point which is very interesting—the matter of cement which we will discuss a little later.

In the area of Mexico and Central America alone, researchers generally agree that there are 2,000 sites of ancient people known to science today. (See page 3 of *The Americas Before Columbus*.) I have been in much of this country. I have tramped the jungle trails; I have taken over 4,000 pictures in Kodachrome of many of the ancient ruins of the South American area, the Central American area, and the North American area. I have thrilled as I have gone into the cities of these ancient people. We read that science as yet has not been able to translate any place name or personal name among all these ruins. I want you to remember that, because when we get to some of these names later, we will find that there is much controversy as to how they should be pronounced. Some are Indian names, some Spanish, some were dreamed up by obscure people. Farnsworth tells us that since scientific researchers have not even been able to translate any place or any personal names, "consequently, all names of cities used in modern treatises on the Mayan civilization have been coined by moderns."

In the meantime, authorities generally agree to this extent (Here is our point). "There were at least **two separate and distinct migrations from Asia to the New World...** one known as Archaic, about 4,000 years ago." (Page 3, *The Americas Before Columbus.*) If we subtract 4,000 years from our current year of 1954, we come to 2,046 B.C.—scientists have already pinpointed the first migration as being at the time of the Tower of Babel or Confusion of Tongues. Do you know that if scientists could translate the names of these immigrant people of whom they speak, they would call them Jaredites?

Some authoritative researchers, according to Farnsworth, go on to say that "the other migration, known as the Mayan-Toltec migration, occurred about 600B.C. The Mayan civilization continued to flourish until it reached its highest point between the second and fifth centuries after Christ." Note that—"between the second and fifth centuries after Christ." The year 421 A.D., the *Book of Mormon* tells us, was the last time the Prophet Moroni wrote on the plates, but actually the last great battle took place about the year 385 A.D.—"between the second and fifth centuries after Christ."

Now listen to what the scientists say about something that happened right after this: "Sometime after this a great catastrophe took place which almost wiped out this ancient civilization and left it in the condition the Spaniards under Cortez, and his followers found it." (*The Americas Before Columbus,* page 3.)

You know this has puzzled the scientists. Why did these Indian people, as we know them today or mis-know them really, walk out of thousands of their cities? They just walked out! There was no evidence of pestilence, no evidence of famine, no evidence of war in the cities. The people just walked out and left city after city after city—cities, in some cases—that once held over a million highly cultured people. They left, and they did not come back. And until you read the *Book of Mormon* story you do not know why. (See *Mormon* 6:2-6.) They were going to make a combined force, a last stand—men and women and children fighting to get a decision as to which side would win, the Lamanites or the Nephites. Which side did win? The Lamanites. And the Nephites, in the main—not entirely, were killed off.

Now let us go back and check it again. Do scientists agree that there were two main groups of people in early times who came to this land? Yes. Do they agree that one of these groups came at the time of the Jaredite nation? Yes. And do they agree that the other people came at the time of the Nephite-Lamanite nation? Yes. Isn't it interesting that they call the second people the Mayan-Toltecs—two names. If they could translate those names correctly, what would they call them? Nephite-Lamanites.

Alright, now the **SECOND CLAIM** of the *Book of Mormon* which we will consider: The *Book of Mormon* tells us that the Nephites brought with them from the old continent certain records known as the **BRASS PLATES OF LABAN.** These must have been very important, for in securing these plates, a man lost his life. Nephi, the son of Lehi, had never shed the blood of man, and he shirked from the responsibility of slaying Laban. But the spirit said to him:

> Behold the Lord slayeth the wicked to bring forth his right-eous purposes. It is better that one man should perish than that a nation should dwindle and perish in unbelief.
>
> *1 Nephi 4:13*

The brass plates must have been a very important record for the people—a record which would keep them from "dwindling in unbelief."

> For behold, Laban hath the record of the Jews and also a genealogy of thy forefathers, and they are engraven upon plates of brass.

Wherefore, the Lord hath commanded me that thou and thy brothers should go unto the house of Laban, and seek the records, and bring them down hither into the wilderness.

1 Nephi 3:3-4

And the *Book of Mormon* goes on to tell us of the things written on the brass plates, so that we have every reason to believe that the record was similar to the *Old Testament,* up to, but not including, the capture of Jerusalem by the Babylonians. (See *1 Nephi 5:10-15.*) When this statement was read by some of our friends in other churches, in their pulpits they shouted, "Blasphemy!" They said, "You mean to tell us that those heathen savages had a record in ancient times similar to the *Old Testament?"* All in the world our Latter-day Saint people could tell them in 1830, when the book came off the press, was: "We believe that book. We have a testimony of its truth." But at that time they could not have proven the statement that these people had records similar to the *Old Testament.* Today Latter-day Saints do not need to prove it because science has done it for us.

Let us go to page 41 of *The Americas Before Columbus* and read a quotation from DeRoo. He says,

> That man was created in the image of God was a part of Mexican belief, says Kingsborough. Another point of coincidence with the scripture record is found in the Mexican Goddess "Ciocoatl" or serpent women whom the Aztec addressed as Our Lady and Mother, the first goddess who brought forth, who bequeathed the sufferings of childbirth to women as a tribute of death; by whom sin came into the world. In all this we see much to remind us of the mother of the human family.

Where did they get this information, if indeed they did not have such a record as they claimed to have had? And the Indians told the first Christian ministers who came among them many of these stories when they were first able to understand each other in sign language.

As further evidence that the ancient inhabitants of the Americas had a knowledge and record of the *Old Testament*, let us read on page 26 of *The Americas Before Columbus*, the quote of Alvin Colton, a man who lived with many of the Indian tribes and learned many of their legends:

> The story of the flood is widely current among the American Indians. A man named Noach *(notice how close—not Noah, but Noach)* with certain other people, escaped in a boat filled with various animals and birds. A **rainbow** is the sign that this will not happen again.

Do you know that there is no other place except the Bible where the story is told of how the rainbow was placed in the sky as a promise from God to his children that he would never again destroy the earth by flood? The Old Testament is the only place it has been recorded, and yet the Indian people knew of this rainbow story when the first Christian ministers came among them.

Mr. Colton's statement continues:

> In course of time a tower was erected for the purpose of reaching the clouds, but the god, incensed at this presumption, destroyed the tower, confused the language of the day and disbursed the people.
>
> Jacob and his twelve sons are found in the legends of the American Indians. Some of the tribes "used to build an altar of twelve stones in memory of a great ancestor of theirs who had twelve sons." They had traditions that all Indian tribes descended from one man who had twelve sons. *(What was Jacob's other name? Israel. He had twelve sons, and they became the heads, in their prime condition at least, of the twelve tribes of Israel. The Indians knew this background of the* Old Testament *story.)* That this man was a notable and renowned prince, having great dominion; and that the Indians, his posterity, will yet recover that same dominion and influence.

Isn't that interesting? The *Book of Mormon* says that in the latter-days when the Lamanites (American Indians) once again accept and live the gospel of Jesus Christ, they will become a white and delightsome people and that through them every nation of the world will be blessed. Yes, the Indians had that legend. Yes, they had brass plates as described, a record of the old continent.

Let us read a quotation from DeRoo on page 65 of the book. Then we'll read a statement of Kingsborough, the granddaddy of the American continent archaeological group, who is quoted and requoted perhaps more than any other archaeologist. DeRoo says:

> The Indian narrated to him how, long ago, the Otomis were in possession of a book, handed down from father to son and guarded by persons of importance whose duty it was to explain it... For the sake of reverence, they did not turn the leaves with their hands, but with a tiny stick kept along with the book for that purpose. The friar having asked the Indian what the contents of the volume were and its teachings, the old man could not give the details, but said that, were it in existence yet, it would be evident that the teachings of that book and the preaching of the friar were one and the same. *(Now note this interesting piece of evidence.)* But the venerable heirloom had perished **in the ground, where its guardians had buried it.**

Yes, of course, they had a record similar to the Old Testament. Now on page 18, a quote from Kingsborough:

> I cannot fail to remark that one of the arguments which persuades me to believe that this nation descends from the Hebrews is to see the knowledge they have of the book of *Genesis.*

In another treatise Kingsborough, also on page 18, tells us about the *Borgian Manuscript,* found in the jungle country buried under centuries of debris, with no possible chance that it could have been tampered with by modern-day man.

A very remarkable representation of the ten plagues, which God sent on Egypt, occurs in the eleventh and twelfth pages of the Borgian Manuscript. Moses is there painted, holding up in his left hand his rod, which became a serpent; and, with a furious gesture, calling down the plagues upon the Egyptians. These plagues were frogs, locusts, lice, flies, etc., all of which are represented in the pages referred to; but the last and most dreadful were the thick darkness which overspread Egypt for three days, and the death of the firstborn of the Egyptians...

Where did these people get these ideas if they did not have some record of the *Old Testament* events and peoples?

The *Book of Mormon* makes a **THIRD CLAIM,** which is: **JESUS CHRIST APPEARED ON THIS CONTINENT** after his crucifixion and resurrection on the old continent. Let us turn to *3 Nephi, chapter 11.* I wish that we had someone with the talent of Sid Grauman. Some of you may have seen, in times of the past, Grauman's prologues in Hollywood. If you saw the one of *King of Kings,* I know that you will remember it all the days of your life. Someone needs to depict this event—one of the most marvelous things that ever depict this event—one of the most marvelous things that ever happened on the earth—the coming of Jesus Christ to this continent. Remember the background, three hours of terrible destruction while the prophets of this continent testified Christ was being crucified on the old continent. Then the three days and nights of darkness, the darkness so dense and damp that they could not light any kind of fire. Then came the quietude in which they did not dare speak to each other. A long period of unknown time followed, then a voice came out of the heavens. The third time they heard the voice, they understood some words. Let us in fact go to the *Book of Mormon:*

> Behold my Beloved Son, in whom I am well pleased, in whom I have glorified my name—hear ye him.
> And it came to pass, as they understood they cast their eyes

up again towards heaven; and behold, they saw a Man descending out of heaven; and he was clothed in a white robe; and he came down and stood in the midst of them; and the eyes of the whole multitude were turned upon him, and they durst not open their mouths, even one to another, and wist not what it meant, for they thought it was an angel that had appeared unto them.

And it came to pass that he stretched forth his hand and spake unto the people, saying:

Behold, I am Jesus Christ, whom the prophets testified shall come into the world.

3 Nephi 11:7-10

Can you visualize this with me? Two thousand five hundred people saw Him descending out of heaven. (See *3 Nephi 17:25*.)

...and the eyes of the whole multitude were upon him, and they durst not open their mouths, even one to another, and wist not what it meant, for they thought it was an angel that had appeared to them.

3 Nephi 11:8

Then this personage identified himself, "Behold I am Jesus Christ whom the prophets testified shall come into the world." *(3 Nephi 11:10.)* Next, He invited them to come forth and thrust their hands into the hole in his side and feel the prints of the nails in his hands and feet, "...that you may know that I am the God of Israel and the God of the whole earth, and have been slain for the sins of the world." *(3 Nephi 11:14.)* And then, one by one, all the men, women, and children did go and "did see with their eyes and did feel with their hands and did bear record, that it **was** he, of whom it was written by the prophets, that should come." *(3 Nephi 11:15.)* And these people did testify of this event from generation to generation that the God of Israel of whom their prophets had testified **did come** to them.

Bancroft says in his *Native Races* that you just cannot find a tribe of Indians today which does not have the legend among their people of the Great White God who was the Son of God, who came to live with their ancient people and taught them his beautiful gospel.

I talked with an old Indian, a "Patriarch" the guide called him, way out a thousand miles by jungle trail from Mexico City, in his little hut in Yucatan. With no warning my guide said, "You **tell** him the story you told me about our gold Bible." And in broken Spanish, with the help of the guide, I told him briefly (in an hour's time) the story of his ancient religion coming from the "golden Bible." He listened intently; then when I got to the story where Christ came walking down out of heaven to live among them— the Son of God who was a God in his own right, who died, was crucified on a cross on the old continent, during which time there was a great destruction on this continent for three hours—the old man's eye filled with tears and he started to nod, and he said **"Si, es verdad. Si, es correcto!"** (Yes, that's true. Yes, that's correct!) From then on, while I told the rest of the story, from time to time he would nod and say the same thing. Then for two hours I sat in his hut listening to the legends of his Indian people. It was marvelous to me, of course. He told me they **did** have the legend that their people would become great again like their forefather who had twelve sons, *(Father Israel)* but not until **after** their true ancient religion came back to them again.

Point after point of his story tied in perfectly with the *Book of Mormon* story.

And yet in the year 1830, when this statement was read in the *Book of Mormon*—that Christ had been among the people—again the LDS people heard the opposing churches shout, "Blasphemy!" The churches said, "Do you mean to tell us that the Son of God himself came to these savages?" All that our Latter-day Saints could say in 1830, was "Well, that is what the book says, and we have confidence and faith in that book." They could not have proven it with then existing evidence, but today the evidence is complete.

Before we go on to more quotations from the scientists let me tell you about something first: Last fall my wife (mother of my six children) and I went on a second honeymoon to end all honeymoons. We went down through all of the South American and the Central American countries, visiting every island of the Caribbean Sea enroute, in and out of twenty-nine nations, and covering 38,500 miles. We had an excuse to go on this trip because our son, Jack, Jr., was just getting off his mission in Brazil, and we had promised to meet him in Rio de Janeiro.

I had wanted to take Jack, Jr. and my wife, Lerona (whom I call my "good-looking girl friend") through all the major ancient ruins down there while getting some additional colored pictures and having a good vacation at the same time. Boy, were we having fun! But when we arrived in Brazil, the "honeymoon" was over! I just **thought** I was on a vacation. When we arrived in Rio and met my son, he had *Book of Mormon* lecture engagements scheduled for me all over South America. The vacation ended very abruptly.

In attempting to cover a little bit of the material we have covered in *The Trial of the Stick of Joseph,* for those people in South and Central America, we combined the three lectures, believe it or not, into one and called it: "Christ Came to the Americas." We found the people completely captivated with the idea that Jesus Christ had been among the people in early times on this continent, and they were amazed! Then, as we got deeper and deeper into Indian country, we found no consternation whatsoever; because the Indians **knew** that Christ had been among their forefathers and had taught their people his beautiful gospel.

But this idea of Christ's ministry in America **did** cause many of the other church groups great alarm in the year 1830, when they found the *Book of Mormon* claimed that Jesus Christ had lived with people, had taught them His gospel, and had indeed set up His church and appointed twelve disciples to follow up with the work on this continent.

Now let us get back to the "experts" again. Turn to *The Americas Before Columbus*, page 36, and read a quote from Kingsborough:

> The legendary Christ of America performed miracles and taught Christian doctrines. Rosales' *History of Chile* declares, "A wonder man had come to that country, who performed many miracles, cured the sick with water, kindled fire at a breath, caused it to rain and their crops and grain to grow, healing at once the sick, giving sight to the blind."

Another quote from Kingsborough, on that same page:

> The Aztecs have a tradition of a God suffering and crucified named Quetzalcoatl, and of one preceding Him to prepare the way and call them to repentance. Tezcaltlipoca offered Him a cup, calling Him "Mu son," of His unwillingness to taste and weeping bitterly after having drunk its contents; forsaking temporal kingdoms for spiritual, being called away by the Father. At His departure there were four earthquakes. **He promised to return again** and redeem His people.

Have you ever stopped to wonder why it was that Cortez and a mere handful of people were able to subjugate millions of Indians? Have you ever wondered why he was able to write his very name in blood all across the face of Mexico? I have some of the personal writings of Las Casas the first bishop of Chiapas. He says that as he writes, tears are in his eyes, and he tells us, "Up to my time alone, in this area alone, Cortez has murdered in cold blood over fifteen million Indians, because they refused to accept a form of Christianity which they say is even less perfect than their own, and yet they know they have degenerated from the original."

Now why did the Indians allow such slaughter? I know an Indian chief very personally who is a direct descendant of

Montezuma, and he has some of the personal writings of Montezuma. In these writings it is made very clear that the Indians could have snuffed out Cortez any time they wanted, until he turned Indian tribe against Indian tribe or Indian against Indian. Why then did they let him live? Why did they let him commit such atrocities? **Because they believed he was the White God returning,** even as their forefathers had promised He would return to them! Finally I asked the old Indian "Patriarch" in Yucatan, "Were not there any of the Indian people who finally believed he could not possibly be a God, and do the terrible things he did to your people?" He said, "Yes, many finally believed he could not possibly be a God, but they also had the legend from their ancient people that a white race had to conquer us before our true religion would come back to us again." And so even those who finally believed that he was not the returning White God would not turn against him, knowing that they had to be conquered by a white race of people. They knew the God of their forefathers would come back, and their true religion would come back prior to His coming.

On page 41 of our reference text, Farnsworth quotes from P. DeRoo regarding the possibility that Jesus Christ did come to this land in early times.

It is not our intention to exaggerate the importance of these coincidences of ancient American traditions with the history of our Saviour; but their Christian origin and Christian meaning could hardly be called in question, if we should happen to find, alongside with them, among the same aborigines, such emblems, doctrines, and practices as evidently are Christian exclusively. Who will deny that, if the cross, the peculiar symbol of Christianity, should be found in Yucatan, it would stamp as Christian the tradition of its inhabitants, according to which they believed that their son-god (*not s-u-n god, but s-o-n god*) born of a virgin, died crucified?

Of course Jesus Christ had been with them and taught them beautiful things, and they heard from his own lips wonderful stories.

Now turn over the page to quote from Brinton on page 42.

> We thus arrived, still in primitive conditions, to such personal ideals as Quetzalcoatl among the Aztecs of whom it was said in their legends that he was a majestic presence, chaste in life, averse to war, wise and generous in actions, and delighting in the cultivation of the arts of peace; or as we see among the Peruvians, in their culture hero Tonopa, of whose teachings a Catholic writer of the sixteenth century says, "So closely did they resemble the precepts of Jesus, that nothing was lacking in them but His name and that of His Father."

We cannot translate proper names, can we? Otherwise they would have the name of Jesus Christ and God the Father in these ancient ruins.

Yes, Christ **was** with these people, and he **did** give them these beautiful teachings.

Now, the **FOURTH CLAIM**—here is another so-called fantastic claim of the *Book of Mormon*. The book tells us that they not only **WROTE ON GOLD** but that the people wrote **IN REFORMED EGYPTIAN** hieroglyphics and **HEBREW**. "Whoever heard of people writing on gold?" many people cried n the year 1830. "How fantastic can you get?" they said when "Joe" Smith, as they called him, was supposed to have a golden record of these ancient Hebrew people written in a form of Egyptian hieroglyphics. And yet the record continues to maintain that they did write on gold:

> And for a testimony that the things that they had said are true they have brought twenty-four plates, which are filled with engravings, and they are of pure gold.
>
> *Mosiah 8:9*

Now we turn to Mormon who, you will remember, was one of the great prophets of the book, and also the man who abridged a great portion of the history of these people. Speaking of the language they used in writing the book, he wrote:

> And now, behold, we have written this record according to our knowledge, in the characters which are called among us the reformed Egyptian, being handed down and altered by us, according to our manner of speech.
>
> And if our plates had been sufficiently large we should have written in Hebrew; but the Hebrew hath been altered by us also...
>
> *Mormon 9:32-33*

For years these statements puzzled scientists. They are still puzzled by some of them. Picture, if you will, poor old Professor Marett, an archaeologist, pacing back and forth in front of a tomb that he excavated in Monte Alban, in the tops of the mountains in the lower Mexican country. He is wringing his hands and saying, "It cannot be! How can a people be Egyptian at the same time that they are Hebrew, and be of all places, on this continent?" He had not read the story of the *Old Testament* recently, of the Hebrew-born boy Joseph—the boy of the coat of many colors—a son of Israel. He had not read how Joseph became a leader of one of the tribes of Israel, a branch of which came to this continent, according to the *Book of Mormon* story. Marett had not read recently in the *Bible* how this Hebrew boy went down into Egypt, was sold by his brothers into slavery and became, with the help of God, the literal and veritable head of the Egyptian government. For the time came that Pharaoh said to Joseph, "...according unto thy word shall all my people be ruled...I have set thee over all the land of Egypt." (See *Genesis 41:40,41*.) And then during the years of famine, you remember, his family came down to Egypt to get food. This is a story in itself. When the Pharaoh heard of Joseph's family starving in the land of Canaan, he said unto Joseph:

...Say unto thy brethren, This do ye; lade your beasts, and go, get you unto the land of Canaan;

And take your father and your households, and come unto me: and I will give you the good of the land of Egypt, and ye shall eat the fat of the land.

Now thou art commanded, this do ye; take your wagons out of the land of Egypt for your little ones, and for your wives, and bring your father, and come.

Also regard not your stuff; for the good of the land of Egypt is yours.

Genesis 45:17-20

Living there in Egypt, the Hebrew people, particularly those of the tribe of Joseph, would learn the arts and sciences of the Egyptians and they naturally would learn the language of the Egyptians, but of course they would also cling, as do all Hebrews, to their own ancient language and customs.

This story is the only answer in the world to the problem the archaeologist Marett had as to how a people could be Egyptian at the same time they were Hebrew, and be on this continent.

Let us see if these people did write on gold. On page 65 of our reference book, we turn to a quotation from *The Goldsmith's Art In Ancient Mexico,* by Saville: "Padre Gay mentions...that the Mexican Indians sold to some European antiquarians very thin plates of gold, evidently worked with the hammer, which their ancestors had been able to preserve, and on which were engraved ancient hieroglyphs."

Yes, of course, they wrote on gold and wrote in ancient Egyptian hieroglyphics but their Egyptian writing was not like the most ancient Egyptian nor was it like modern Egyptian. It was as though some people had come from the very ancient Egyptian area, and had drifted from the original in the characters of their writing and in their language, as Mormon said. That is what is found today on this continent—the reformed hieroglyphics of the Egyptians, but in the manner of "speaking" of the Hebrews.

T.A. Willard, quoted on page 140 of the book, tells us that from the sacred well of Chichen Itza, "Many disks of gold were brought up, which are covered with finely-worked figures in repose, while around the outer edges are characters and symbols and sometimes hieroglyphics."

Some critics said to our people in the year 1830, "If it is true that the people of the *Book of Mormon* had an Egyptian background, why don't we find any pyramids on this continent?" In the year 1830, we could not answer that because no pyramids had been found here. Today we have found pyramids all over the face of the land, and **what** pyramids! One is such a giant that you could place the largest pyramid of Egypt down in one corner of its base, set two other pyramids of like size alongside, and still, within the base of this one American pyramid, you would have enough room left for a ball field. This is the giant pyramid of Cholula. Five miles of tunnels have been built inside of it by the Mexican government so that anyone who pays the price of admission may go inside and see what makes a pyramid tick. Of course, pyramids have been found on this continent.

On page 22 of *The Americas Before Columbus*, Jones, the archaeologist is sure these ancient Americans are Egyptians and then on page 18 he is just as certain they are Hebrew. So he is in trouble and he says, "How can this be? They are Egyptians one minute and Hebrews the next."

From his *Ancient America*, as quoted by Farnsworth on page 22, Jones offers this testimony:

> And as if in direct copy of the Egyptian, we have shown that the size of the Pyramidal base at Copan* is identical with that of the great Pyramid of the Nile—while that at Cholula, in Mexican America, is **exactly twice** the base measurement. It is scarcely possible that these dimensions should have been accidental in construction.

On page 18 of *The Americas Before Columbus*, this same researcher, Jones, represents many scientists who have found both the Egyptian and Hebrew background.

> Many other religious customs and ceremonies exist... strictly in analogy with the race of Abraham; but enough has been brought forward in this volume to propose these *(as we believe)* unanswerable questions: "If they are not of the Lost Tribes of Israel, who are they?"
>
> "What nation of ancient history can claim and identify those customs and observances as their own, if not the Hebrew?"

Writings in Hebrew have now been found. Down in one tomb at Monte Alban, Professor Marett found artifacts and sculpture work, which were, on the one hand, absolutely **Egyptian** and he gives us many reasons why. Then, on the other hand, he found other artifacts and sculpture work in the same tomb, made out of the same materials and, as nearly as he could tell, done by the same artisans, which were "just as positively **Hebrew.**"

And so as I mentioned before, we find the archaeologist Marett in trouble. Let us read a statement of Marett for a closing thought on this particular point. This is also in our reference book, page 22:

> Far from throwing any light on the origin of the early Mexican and the source of his amazing knowledge of sculpture, astronomy, architecture, and durable colors, and his cultural development, this marvelous collection of antiquities only adds to the mystery. The idols and images exhibited here show features of Indian types; some are unmistakably Hebrew; other are certainly Egyptian.

Yes, they did write on gold; they did write in Egyptian; and they could have written and did write, in many cases, in Hebrew.

The **FIFTH CLAIM** which seemed ridiculous in the *Book of*

Mormon was that these early American inhabitants **BUILT** cities, highways, and building **WITH CEMENT.** Now I don't know if there were any general contractors back in 1830, but if there were, I am sure some of them who read the *Book of Mormon* must have said: "Well, now, there are just lots of things in that book I can believe, but here you are talking about my special field of construction. Do you mean to tell me in our enlightened day and age of 1830, when we barely know what the material cement is, when we can build nothing with it, that these heathen savages *(as they kept calling them)* back in the dim ages were able to build giant highways stretching from sea to sea and coast to coast, and tremendous cities, and mammoth buildings, with the use of cement? That is ridiculous!" And all in the world our people could say in the year 1830, again was, "We have faith in that book. We believe it." But in that year, we could not have proven that the ancient people built with cement.

Regarding the use of cement the *Book of Mormon* says:

> And there being but little timber upon the face of the land *(northward)*, nevertheless the people who went forth became exceeding expert in the working of cement...
>
> *Helaman 3:7*

> And thus they did enable the people **in the land northward** that they might build many cities... of cement.
>
> *Helaman 3:11*

It's real interesting that we find no evidence of the use of cement in South America, but the minute you go north of the "narrow neck" in the Panamanian area into the **land northward,** cement shows up in all their construction work. The ancient cement was far superior to any cement we have today.

Let us look at the testimony of one of today's experts: Farnsworth quotes from T.A. Willard again on page 38. Every time I read this I get a little kick out of it because it reminds me of an experience I had on my hands and knees polishing out cement the hard way.

Willard tells the story of John MacAdam, a Scottish engineer, who lived and died honestly believing that he had invented a system of road making, called by us even today, "MacAdam" road. But over two thousand years before John MacAdam was born, we are told that road makers were using those same principles in Yucatan.

> ...roads were built in Yucatan that embodied all his sound principles of road making. And MacAdam lived and died without ever having heard of them... The thoroughness and good engineering of their construction rival the famous roads of the Roman empire or of present-day highways.
>
> In ancient times Chichen Itza and all the great and lesser cities of the Yucatan peninsula, were linked by a network of smooth, hard-surfaced highways...this land... once had the best roads on earth...

The old roads, each and every one **went down to bedrock** and upon that solid foundation was built up a ballast of broken limestone, with the larger stones at the bottom. (That means that they went down **fifty and sixty feet,** in some cases, before they started building back up with the "larger stones at the bottom," and so forth.) As the surface of the road was reached, smaller stones were used and the crevices were filled in. The whole face of the road was then given a smooth hard coating of **mortar cement...** Mortar or cement was then applied in a thin coating and when this had hardened sufficiently, gangs of stout-muscled laborers, armed with smooth, fine-grained polishing stones, rubbed the plastic surface until it became compacted into a polished flatness almost as smooth-coated as tile and nearly as hard.

When Mr. Willard wrote this description of the ancient roads, he did not know that the scientists would find over 4,000 miles of **one continuous highway** in Central America alone, every inch of it covered with this fine quality cement. I cannot even visualize enough men down on their hands and knees to polish that tremendous cement highway with fine polishing stones. When I was in the bishopric of the Monrovia Ward and I had the Mutual Improvement Association under my supervision, the bishop called me up one day and said, "Jack, how would you like to come down to the church and get some of these scouts to rub out some names they wrote in the fresh concrete down here?" So I went down with some of these "fine polishing stones," and on my hands and knees, with those fellows, we tried to rub out the names, and it was only a few hours after they had been written. We had a dickens of a time. After that experience, I cannot even visualize polishing by hand 4,000 miles of highway! Maybe the ancient people used machinery to trowel and polish their cement highways. The *Book of Mormon* says they had machinery, you know.

Since nearly every Kodachrome slide I'll show you in our next session, taken in any of the ancient cities lying north of the "narrow neck" will give **visual** proof of the use of cement, we will not take more time on this claim now.

The **SIXTH CLAIM** of the *Book of Mormon* was that these early Americans had excellent tools. This was another thing that amazed the public, and still is amazing even to some scientists. The *Book of Mormon* tells us that those people not only made tools, but they were also able to make **HARDENED COPPER TOOLS.** In the year 1830 a great man in the field we now call metallurgy may have said, "There are many things in that book that I can believe, but now you are talking in my specialized field, and any fool knows that you cannot harden copper." Well, in the year 1830, we could not do it, and we cannot do it yet - not pure copper—it is a lost art. But the Egyptians used to be able to do it. In 1830 no evidence had been found to prove this so-called ridiculous statement, but today, did you know that there have been found on this continent, north of the "narrow neck" of land alone, over 10,000 ancient copper tools of these people besides the thousands found in South America? A fascinating sidelight is that when they check with the "carbon 14 test," they have never found one of those copper tools in a city dating back prior to 600 years before Christ. And it was only the Nephite-Lamanite people who claimed to be able to harden copper, and they came 600 years before Christ.

Before turning to our next reference in the *Book of Mormon*,—*Jarom, verse 8*, I want to tell you a story about this reference. A young member of the armed forces wrote to me from overseas and said "Bishop West, in your *Book of Mormon* lectures you gave us a reference of *Jarom, verse 8*, but you failed to give the chapter." I wrote back and said, "My dear young friend I think if you'll look again, you'll see that **there are no chapters** in *Jarom*—just verses." He airmailed another letter and said, "I'll bet my face is so red that it shows clear across the ocean. I promise you I'll become more familiar with the *Book of Mormon*." I humbly pray that we will all become more familiar with the "Four Standard Works" of the Church—the *Bible*, the *Book of Mormon*, the *Doctrine and Covenants* and *The Pearl of Great Price*. I get real concerned about so many of our people reading "commentaries" when they haven't read the "Four Standard Works." Everybody, it seems is writing a book these days and I think its wonderful to read commentary books if we do it as a means of encouraging the **more careful, prayerful and studious reading of the scriptures** upon which the "commentaries" are based. Well, that was quite a dissertation!

Let us now turn briefly to *Jarom verse 8*. May I **again** admonish you always to read the "Four Standard Works" of the Church first, **really study** them and make their beautiful teachings a part of you lives, and then, if you have time, by all means read the commentaries and lectures, such as these. If we are honest with ourselves, I am sure we will admit that too many of our LDS people have not read the *Book of Mormon*, the *Bible*, the *Doctrine and Covenants*, and *The Pearl of Great Price* from cover to cover, even though they have read many commentaries on the "Four Standard Works." Do not let that happen to you.

Now to Jarom:

> And we multiplied exceedingly, and spread upon the face of
> the land, and became exceedingly rich in gold, and in silver, and
> in precious things, and in fine workmanship of wood, in build-
> ings, and in machinery, and also in iron and **copper**, and brass
> and steel, making all manner of **tools** of every kind...
>
> *Jarom verse 8*

Here is our point, "and **copper,** and brass, and steel, **making
all manner of tools...**" This was an amazing statement in the year
1830, and it still sounds fantastic, except in the light of what we
have found. Were they able to harden copper? You bet they were.
Let us turn, for instance, to page 140 of *The Americas Before
Columbus.* Farnsworth quotes Bradford, who tells us that after he
had seen some of the articles which these people had apparently
carved quite easily—some of them emerald, one of our hardest
stones—he was amazed, and he was assured in his own thinking
that they must have had tools of marvelous quality.

> The distinguished traveler just mentioned from the observa-
> tion of the great perfection of these sculptures, was induced to
> believe that **tools of copper** had been used in their formation...
> this conjecture has been justified, by the discovery of an ancient
> Peruvian chisel, found at Villacamba, consisting of ninety-four
> parts of copper and six of tin. Some of the articles found in the
> mounds are also composed of **hardened copper;** and Dr. Meyen,
> in speaking of the collection of antiquities in the Museum at
> Lima, says "the **ancient weapons are of copper** and some are of
> exquisite manufacture."

Eighteen miles south of the beautiful city of Lima, is the ancient
city called Pachacamac, right in the heart of the great desert extend-
ing along the coast of Peru. The whole coastline of Peru is just as
much a desert as the Sahara. From the ocean back an average of

sixty-five miles to the tops of the Andes we find this desert condition. Down in this desert country, at the Pachacamac ruins, a grave was opened and out of the grave were taken some copper tools. Many other copper tools were taken out of other graves.

It was there that I met Bill Salazar, an archaeologist in Peru. Bill had some of the copper tools of the ancient people, which he had dug out of Pachacamac. It is getting to be almost impossible for an individual to buy any of these ancient articles. You have to agree to put them in a museum or establish that you are connected with some museum. I said to Bill, "I would surely like to have one of those copper chisels, Bill. Would you even consider selling one to me?" "Well, maybe." So I got a little chisel. It is about six inches long and about two inches wide. It is shaped very much like our present day chisels except that it comes to a very fine point instead of a very blunt point as do our hard chisels. I asked him if he had a file, and he said, "Yes," and grinned. Well, he gave me the file and I filed through the heavy green oxide coating quite readily, but when I hit the point of the metal itself the file just skidded. I grinned at him. He grinned back and said, "You know, don't you?" I said, "Yes, I do know." He said that some of the hardest metal found anywhere in the world is in the almost pure copper tools of the ancient inhabitants of this continent. I bought that chisel for $10, and what Bill Salazar did not know was that I would have "mortgaged one of my Cadillacs" for it.

I thought I would have a little fun, so I went down to a hardware store in Lima and asked a salesman in my very best Spanish (which was difficult for him to understand), "Do you have a real good file? I want the best." "Oh, **si, senor,**" he had the best file in Peru, so he brought it out, and I bought it. I went back to the hotel and I worked on one side of this copper chisel quite a while and was doing nothing more than just polishing it. I could not begin to cut it with the very best file I could find. I took the file back to the store, and I said to him, "**Es malo.**" I told him I wanted the best, not the worst, he had. And so I said, "See," and he tried it, and it just skidded like it was on a piece of glass. And he said, "**Es verdad, es muy malo.**" ("That's right, it's very bad.") He took it back. I did not ask him to get me another file, but he insisted that he get another file, and of course it did the same thing. Yes, many of these ancient tools were so hard that our best files will not even scratch them.

Immediately after my return from my most recent trip to South America, I read this fascinating article. It made me feel regretful, however, because I was in Lima while this was going on, and did not know about it. *Time Magazine* reported:

> The thirty-one year old patient lay in an up-to-date operating room in Lima, Peru, surrounded by sterile gadgets and the paraphernalia of modern anesthesia. At hand to forestall infection, were ultra-modern antibiotics. Flanking the patient were two of Peru's most distinguished surgeons, Drs. Francisco Graña Reyes and Esteban Rocca. But their instruments were bronze chisels and saws made of obsidian *(volcanic glass)*, which were 2,000 years old when Francisco Pizarro conquered Peru.
>
> Tightly wound around the patient's head was a three-layer bandage tourniquet such as Inca and pre-Inca surgeons used. *(Did you know they had surgeons?)* With the bronze chisel and **copper** hammer, Graña and Rocca cut a hole in the left side of the patient's skull, and cleaned out a blood clot *(the result of an injury)* that had been pressing against his brain and had robbed him of the power of speech. They replaced the piece of skull and sewed up the scalp. The whole operation had taken fourteen minutes. **The ancient surgical instruments were then sent back to the National Museum of Archaeology.** Last week the doctors examined their patient, told him he could go back to his work as a cabinetmaker this week.
>
> The Lima surgeon's feat was no idle trick. For years they had studied ancient skulls, instruments, and bandages, and had practiced using the museum relics in autopsies. After their first use on a live patient, Dr. Graña was delighted. The operation proved, he said, that **the ancients' tools and methods were as good as the**

moderns' and in some ways perhaps better. *(Is not that amazing?)* For the future, he foresaw wider use of the tourniquet bandage, which had given him an almost bloodless field of operation. And he thinks another pre-Inca wrinkle may prove useful: flexible bronze needles, which the surgeon can bend when putting in stitches.

Time Magazine, October 26, 1953

I saw case after case of hardened copper instruments in museum after museum. Yes, of course, they had hardened copper.

Now, the **SEVENTH CLAIM,** The *Book of Mormon* claims that these ancient people **HAD MACHINERY AND WHEELS.** Remember *Jarom verse 8*, told us that. In *3 Nephi 3:22*, and many other places we are told of chariots. They certainly knew the use of wheels. Yet when scientists in 1830 heard that the *Book of Mormon* told about the machinery of the ancient people on this continent, they said. "Why, that could not possibly be true! They did not even understand the use of wheels." They reminded us that the first white men who came to this continent saw and old Indian buck (the smart old fellow) condescending to lift two sticks on his squaw's back. All of their worldly goods were lashed to those sticks, and then the buck went off through the forest and looked over his shoulder and said, "Ug," which meant, "Come on, squaw." She, not knowing any better, followed, **dragging** all their worldly goods behind her **on the point of two sticks.** So the scientists reminded our people that these Indians did not even know the use of the wheel, the very basis of machinery. There are some scientists today who still stubbornly believe that the ancient people did not know the use of the wheel.

Well, let us go to some of the testimony. Page 39 of *The Americas Before Columbus* shows us a picture of the very first evidence found on this continent of the use, anciently, of wheels, This photograph is of a child's toy—the body of a coyote, as near as we can tell from the appearance, with four little stone wheels on it. It was found under the streets of Mexico City in a buried city of the Nephite people. Did you know that there was a whole city under Mexico City? The Mexican people were wondering why their buildings were sinking. The great Palaca of Arts had sunk some twelve feet, and they wondered why. They were assuming that there is a marshy condition causing it. They are building now with thirty and forty foot pilasters of reinforced concrete going down into the earth.

A construction crew was drilling at the corner of Guatemala and Argentina streets, right in the heart of Mexico City, for the foundation of a new building. When they got down a few feet below the surface, suddenly their drill dropped down into a cavity in the earth. They could not imagine what had caused this, so they dug down and found a room in one of the giant structures of the ancient people. They dug all around it and found the same fine quality cement that they had found out at the ruins of Teotihuacan and many other places. They found the same angle-slope to the side of the pyramid that they found in the other cities of these ancient people, the same "winged serpent" sculpture and insignia, and many other things, which assured them that it was a city of the Mayan-Toltec people, or the Nephite-Lamanite people as we know them. In the grave of a child in this ruin was found the first evidence of the wheel—the stone toy, with four stone wheels attached.

To continue the story of this ruin under the streets of Mexico City, a lawsuit was filed; in fact, it has not been settled yet. The government insisted that his location be used for an archaeological site, and the owners of the lot insisted that they were going to erect a building on it. While the government people were not looking, the owners went ahead with their drilling. They got down another thirty feet and dropped through again into empty space. So they went down in there and found the remains of an "archaic" city of apparent giant size. And so there have been three cities, not just one, at Mexico City. The lowest one was the Jaredite people; on top of that, after thirty feet of volcanic debris had covered the earlier ruins, a city of the Nephite-Lamanites was built; and finally is Mexico City today.

Some scientists said, "Well, yes, we grant that this child's toy in an ancient grave does show that they understood the use of the wheel, but this is just a toy. We cannot believe, nor will we believe, that they used them for anything but toys, until we see something a lot larger." Then one day on the shores of Lake Titicaca at the place of the Ten Doors in Bolivia, scientists found some ancient wheels that were "larger," and how! I was up in that country, some 16,000 feet high, and I rode down on an Indian autocarril (railroad bus) to an area of about 12,000 elevation on the shores of Lake Titicaca. I saw ruins all the way. On page 94 of Farnsworth's book, we see four giant wheels. Believe me, those are not toys! Stretching, I can reach seven feet, add two more feet to that and you will have the diameter of each of these wheels—nine feet in diameter, sixteen inches wide on the tread of the wheel. The stone is extremely hard, I am told. A strange thing is seen—square holes for the axles instead of round holes.

Scientists have reconstructed, with the help of these wheels, a conveyance, which they think resembles the ancient wagons or transportation units. Now we begin to see why they were so careful to give stability to their roadbeds, by going down to bedrock, so that they could carry tremendous weights over these roads. We learn that they carried weights up to 300 tons with apparent ease, over great distances and over rugged mountains. Scientists believe the ancients used a wood stronger than our iron—wood for axles, and spacers between the two pairs of wheels; and the axles were square on the ends to fit snugly into the square holes, and then rounded and greased in the center. Some of the extremely strong ancient rope (and they were the best rope-makers in the world) was then looped around the axles to form a rope cradle in the middle. Then away they would go with loads up to 300 tons, the wagons being pulled by horses, or elephants.

We brought back pictures of hardened copper cog-wheels, perfectly machined to fit on round shafts and showing signs of tooth wear; we also have a picture of a threaded stone nut which is a "dead ringer" for an octagon nut today, and of very large stone cog-wheels with machined centers. There can be no question that these people had metallic tools and the **use of the wheel,** the basis for machinery.

Now you can turn to many current encyclopedias, and they will tell you of the use of the wheel by these people. When you see some of their buildings, it is self-evident that they must have had such things.

The **EIGHTH CLAIM** of the *Book of Mormon* which we will consider is that these people had **HORSES AND ELEPHANTS.** We read *(Enos, verse 21; Ether 9:17-19)* that these people had horses and elephants, which they used as beasts of burden. It was a fantastic thing to make such a statement in the year 1830 because there was no evidence then that such a thing was true. In fact, some scientists are still a little bit stubborn. It was not until somebody found an arrowhead imbedded in the bone joints of an ancient elephant on this continent that some scientists gave in. They found elephant skeletons at the Brea Tar Pits in Los Angeles. They had found evidence not only of the ancient elephant, but also of the ancient horse. At the great museum in Exposition Park in Los Angeles you can see them if you would like. But even though they found those skeletons by the hundreds all over this continent some scientists still maintained that those animals were not here contemporaneously with man. Then, when they found an arrowhead imbedded in the bone joint of an elephant, they must have scratched their heads and said, "Well, now, let us see. Elephants do not shoot arrowheads at each other!"

The *Book of Mormon* says, regarding the Jaredites:

> Having all manner of fruit, and of grain, and of silks, and of fine linen, and of gold, and of silver, and of precious things;
> And also all manner of cattle, of oxen, and cows, and of sheep, and of swine, and of goats, and also many other kinds of animals, which were useful for the food of man.

And they also had **horses,** and asses, and there were **elephants** and cureloms and cumoms; all of which were useful unto man, and more especially the elephants and cureloms and cumoms.

Ether 9:17-19

Elephants and horses, we are now **certain,** were here. Almost any recent encyclopedia you want to turn to will tell you of the ancient horses and elephants of this continent, but in 1830, the statement sounded amazing. Now, I do not know about cureloms and cumoms. All I know is that there are two other animals in the Brea Tar Pit collection, which were found alongside the elephants and horses. These show signs, they tell us, of having been used as beasts of burden. We have never seen anything like them, but there they are, and maybe they are the cureloms and cumoms.

The **NINTH CLAIM** of the *Book of Mormon* is that anciently there were on this American continent **GREAT CITIES** with **DENSE POPULATION** and **LARGE BUILDINGS.** It was amazing to read these things in the year 1830. We think we are doing pretty well in this day and age when we start the foundation of one or two great buildings in a given city in a year, yet listen to Alma, in the *Book of Mormon:*

And it came to pass that the Nephites began the foundation of a city *(not the foundation of a **building,** the foundation of a **whole city)**,* and they called the name of the city Moroni; and it was by the east sea; and it was on the south by the line of the possessions of the Lamanites.

And they also began a foundation for a city between the city of Moroni and the city of Aaron, joining the borders of Aaron and Moroni; and they called the name of the city, or the land, Nephihah.

And they also began in that same year to build many cities on the north, one in a particular manner, which they called Lehi, which was in the north by the borders of the seashore.

Alma 50:13-15

Isn't that remarkable? Note! In that **same year** they began to build **many cities,** starting the foundations of the entire cities at once!

Notice the dense population these cities had. We are told in the *Book of Mormon* that from sea to sea—from the sea south to the sea north, the sea east to the sea west—there were cities, and that implies there was hardly any area where you could not find cities filled with highly civilized people. But could our people prove in the year 1830 that the ancient people had great cities, dense population and large buildings? Not at all!

Yet as we turn to *The Americas Before Columbus,* we find the proof everywhere we look. There is enough evidence to talk a solid week on any one of these points if we wanted to. It is a fascinating study. If you have not been interested in this thing, get interested in it. It is amazing and fascinating to follow the story of scientific findings on this continent. I am going to use just one quote on this ninth claim. Our time is running short. Look up the other references at your convenience on both the ninth and tenth claims (see the chart for Act III, on page 68 of this publication.) Dr. Sylvanus G. Morley of Carnegie Institute is one of the most careful scientists we have known. He is not in the habit of exaggerating. He is quoted on page 104 of our reference book:

Here in Yucatan a magnificent civilization had been developed. Great cities had flourished on every side. Lofty pyramid-temples and splendid palaces of cut stone, spacious plazas and courts filled with elaborately carved monuments of strange, yet imposing dignity, market places, terraces, causeways, were to be counted, not by the tens and scores, but by hundreds and thousands.

Yes, they are to be counted by the hundreds and thousands. Other references verify this.

The **TENTH CLAIM** of the *Book of Mormon* is that there were many **SUNKEN AND DESTROYED CITIES,** and terrifying destruction on this continent at the time of the crucifixion of Christ. Read about it in *3 Nephi, the 8th and 9th chapters.* Read what happened during those "three hours" of destruction. It's a shocking, revealing account.

Now let us turn to just one quote on this. On page 41 of Farnsworth's book we read from Bancroft again. He not only tells us of the great destruction, which took place on this continent, but he also pinpoints the time of its having taken place. "The sun and moon were eclipsed, the earth shook and the rocks were rent asunder, and many other things and signs happened... This was in the year CeCalli, which the chronology being reduced to our system, proves to be the same date when Christ our Lord suffered, 33 A.D." Isn't that something!

Now, brothers and sisters and friends, I plead with you to read the **Book of Mormon.** Study it; I have hesitated for years to put what I have been giving in lectures in written form because I feard someone would read that and not read the original scripture on which it was based. Read the *Book of Mormon* more carefully than you have heretofore done; be honest with yourself when you ask yourself the question, "Have I read that book from cover to cover?" I want you to be affirmative, read the *Book of Mormon* now! And then read the *Book of Mormon* again and **again,** until you have found and are using the beautiful "blueprint for living" which it contains. I am a very slow reader. I tend to study as I read and to drift into by-paths of thought suggested by the material I am reading—but I can read the book from cover to cover in twenty-six hours. Most readers, if they are fast can read it in eighteen hours. Verify that by reading a page and time yourself, and then multiply that by the number of pages in the book and you will find that I am correct. I have tested it time and time again.

Now, surely out of your lifetime you can spare twenty-six hours even if you are a slow reader, and read that book. Do not let it lie on your shelves gathering dust. Contained within it is the story of Christ's ministry on this earth, on this continent in particular. It has the answers to your personal problems, your family problems, national problems, and international problems.

I testify to you with every ounce of fervor in me, that unless we, as "the salt of the earth," the "leavening" influence, read this book, understand it, are able to teach it, can tell our neighbors about it, and can spread the information throughout the world, the world will be in very great danger. Either we are going to turn to the things of Jesus Christ as we have never done before on the face of the earth, or we are going to be annihilated as a human race.

I humbly pray that we will go to the testimony of that book, that we will never doubt the *Book of Mormon* for a second, that our testimonies will grow and increase as we continue to study it. And this I pray in the name of Jesus Christ. Amen.

Bibliography

Baldwin, John D. *Ancient America.* New York: Harper and Brothers, 1872, p. 176.

Bancroft, Hubert Howe. *Native Races.* 5 vols. 1893. Vol. V, pp. 19-22, 210

Bradford, Alexander W. *American Antiquities.* New York, Boston: Dayton and Saxton,

Saxton and Pierce, 1841, pp. 158-159.

Brinton, Daniel Garrison. *American Hero Myths.* Philadelphia: H.C. Watts and Company, 1882, pp. 145-146.

_____. *Religions of Primitive Peoples.* Philadelphia: H.C. Watts and Company, 1891, p. 251

Charnay, Desire. *Ancient Cities of the New World.* (J. Gonino and Helen S. Conant) New York: Harper and Brothers, 1887, p. 69.

Colton, Alvin. *Origin of the American Indian.* London, 1883.

DeRoo, Peter. *History of America Before Columbus.* Philadelphia, London: J.P. Lippincott Company, 1900, pp. 41, 65.

Encyclopedia Britannica. "Horses, ancient;" "Elephants, ancient." 14th edition. 1929.

Farnsworth, Dewey. *The Americas Before Columbus.* El Paso, Texas: Farnsworth Publishing Col., 1947.

Galatin, Albert. Quoted in Bancroft's *Native Races.* Vol. V, p. 19

Gann, Thomas W. Francis. Maya Cities, *Ancient Cities and Modern Tribes.* New York: Scribner's, 1926-1931, pp. 99-100.

Grãna Reyes, Francisco. "Echo of the Incas." *Time Magazine.* LXII, No. 17 (October 26, 1953), 54-56.

Jones, George. *The History of Ancient America.* New York: Harper and Brothers, 1843, p. 126.

Jordan, Emil. *Americans.* New York: W.W. Norton and Co. Inc., 1939, p. 21.

Kingsborough, Lord. *Mexican Antiquities.* 1829. Vol. VI, p. 401; Vol. VIII, p.3; Scraps, p. 277.

Lee, J. Fitzergald. The Great Migration. 1932, p. 63.

Lowry. Quoted in Schoolcrafts Enthnological Researches. 1853, Vol. 3.

Marett. Archaeological Relics in Mexico. P. 29.

Mason, Gregory. Columbus Came Late. New York, London: The Century Co., 1931, pp. 64, 198.

Morley, Sylvanus G. Introduction to the Study of Maya Hieroglyphs. Washington, D.C.:

Bureau of American Ethnology, 1915. Bulletin 57.

_____. The Inscriptions at Copan. Washington, D.C.: Carnegie Institute, 1920. Publication 219.

Murray, Raymond William. Man's Unknown Ancestors. Milwaukee: Bruce Publishing Co., 1943, pp. 47-49.

Nadaillac, Jean Francois Albert Du Puget, marquis de. (translated by N.C. Amvers and edited by W.H. Dall) *Prehistoric America.* New York: C.P. Putnam, 1884, p. 181.

New Americanized Encyclopedia. "Horses, ancient;" "Elephants, ancient." Vol. V, p. 3197.

Poindexter, Miles. *The Ayar-Incas.* Vols. 1-11. New York: H. Liveright, 1868, 1930, pp. 230-231.

Putnam, Prof. E.W. "Prehistoric Remains of the Ohio Valley," *Century Magazine,* March 1890.

Rosales, *History of Chile.*

Saville, Marshall Howard. *The Goldsmith's Art in Ancient Mexico.* (Museum of the American Indian) New York; Heye Foundation. 1920. p. 175.

Schoolcrafts Enthnological Researches. 1853, Vol. 3.

Spinden, H.J. *Ancient Civilizations of Mexico and Central America.* Handbook Series No. 3. New York: American Museum of Natural History, 1922, pp. 49, 75.

Thompson, Edward Herbert. *People of the Serpent.* Boston, New York: Houghton-Mifflin Co., 1932, p. 228.

Times Encyclopedia and Gazetteer. "Horses, ancient;" "elephants, ancient." Vol. IV.

Willard, Theodore Arthur. *The City of the Sacred Well.* New York: Century Company, 1926, pp. 88-90, 134.